Thomas Cook

TRAVELLERS

BOSNIA, SERBIA & MONTENEGRO

By
TIM CLANCY

Written by Tim Clancy

Original photography by Tim Clancy, Vlado Marinkovic, Munever Salihovic and Carly Calhoun

Editing and page layout by Cambridge Publishing Management Ltd, Unit 2, Burr Elm Court, Caldecote CB23 7NU
Series Editor: Karen Beaulah

Published by Thomas Cook Publishing
A division of Thomas Cook Tour Operations Ltd
Company Registration No. 1450464 England

PO Box 227, The Thomas Cook Business Park,
Coningsby Road, Peterborough PE3 8SB, United Kingdom
E-mail: books@thomascook.com
www.thomascookpublishing.com
Tel: +44 (0)1733 416477

ISBN: 978-1-84157-786-9

Text © 2007 Thomas Cook Publishing
Maps © 2007 Thomas Cook Publishing

Project Editor: Rebecca Snelling
Production/DTP/Editor: Steven Collins

Printed and bound in Italy by: Printer Trento.

Front cover credits, L–R: ©DIOMEDIA/Alamy; ©Lee Foster/Lonely Planet Images; ©Charles Bowman/Alamy
Back cover credits, L–R: ©World Pictures/Photoshot; ©Patrick Horton/Lonely Planet Images

Contents

Introduction

This western Balkans guide covers three countries that are all entirely different, yet somehow rather similar to one another. Bosnia and Herzegovina, Serbia and Montenegro comprised half of the former Yugoslavia. The cultural, natural, political and historical ties of these southern Slav nations transcend many generations. In recent times, however, due to both the war and the collapse of the Berlin Wall, new identities have emerged in the former Yugoslavia, with Bosnia and Herzegovina, Serbia and Montenegro being no exception.

Each country highlighted here has incomparable characteristics. Bosnia and Herzegovina is a country rich in terms of both cultural and natural heritage. It was the heart of the former Yugoslavia, and still boasts the status of being the most ethnically mixed country here, with a diverse Catholic and Orthodox Christian, Muslim and Jewish population. Bosnia is often considered the European crossroads between East and West. As does Montenegro, Bosnia and Herzegovina enjoys both a Mediterranean climate to the south and a continental Alpine one to the north.

To the east lies the largest of the former Yugoslav republics, Serbia. Serbia too has a rich and fascinating history. Similar to the Bosnians, the Serbs are well known for their friendly hospitality – despite the demonisation of them by some of the Western media. Belgrade and Novi Sad surprise most first-time visitors with their charm and vibrancy. The southwest region is more rugged and underdeveloped, but it is endowed with great natural beauty in the areas of Mokra Gora, Tara National Park and Zlatibor.

Montenegro, a tiny nation of just over half a million people, is a rugged and mountainous country with a magnificent stretch of the Adriatic coast. Most of the tourism attractions are based on the coast, with the crystal-clear waters of the Adriatic being a magnet for many Western travellers. The bays, sandy beaches and rustic Mediterranean feel have made tourism the number one industry in the country. The highlands are some of Europe's finest, representing the southernmost extension of the Central Dinaric Alps that stem from its sister range, the Swiss Alps.

What all three countries share is an interesting balance of preserving their old world European lifestyles while

Mostar's Stari Most (old bridge) was reconstructed in 2005

embracing the challenges of newly emerging European nations. In short, this region represents for many a new and exciting destination with a distinct cultural and natural heritage unique to this region. However, you shouldn't expect the tourism catering culture of, say, France, but rather a more raw and authentic tourism experience.

The cities and coastal regions are all rather modern, while the rural and mountain areas maintain their traditional lifestyles and often have simpler tourism catering facilities. Although considerable progress has been made in the tourism industry, particularly in Montenegro, information and customer services are still at a medium level in comparison to well-developed tourism destinations, and you may not always get the information you need. Consequently, you may have to dig a little deeper to uncover the wonders of this region, but it is well worth the effort.

The land

Much of Bosnia and Herzegovina is covered with stunningly beautiful mountains. Perhaps even more remarkable are the ecosystems and vast number of endemic flora and fauna found throughout the country.

Serbia is the largest country in the western Balkans, and this landlocked republic was once the powerhouse of the former Yugoslavia.

Montenegro is the smallest country in the western Balkans, with only 13,800sq km (5,328sq miles) of territory. Nonetheless, over 290km (180 miles) of pristine coastal waters has made it one of the most popular up-and-coming new European destinations.

Bosnia and Herzegovina

It is believed that during the last Ice Age, over 10,000 years ago, the territory of present-day Bosnia and Herzegovina was part of the small green belt where much of Europe's biodiversity survived and, in many instances, thrived.

The long chain of the Southern Alps – the Dinaric Alps – stretches from northwest Croatia through the heart of Bosnia and Herzegovina and into Montenegro. Bosnia is derived from the ancient Indo-European word *bosana*, meaning 'water'. Every corner of this central Balkan state is endowed with a plethora of clean water sources. The river systems are among the most abundant in Europe, with many of the main waterways being potable.

Herzegovina and the Sarajevo region

are dominated by massive mountain ranges, while towards the north of the country the landscape turns from the rugged Alpine peaks to green mountains and rolling hills covered with lush forests and meadows.

The central belt of Bosnia has both rocky mountains and green, rolling hills covered with conifer forests and lined with countless freshwater streams and rivers. Some northern areas are part of the long and agriculturally rich Pannonian plains that extend from Hungary, through Slavonia and Croatia, into the fertile fields of the Sava and Drina river valleys. Stemming from the northwest of the country all the way to Herzegovina are the world's largest karst fields, with deep limestone caves and an intricate system of underground aquifers.

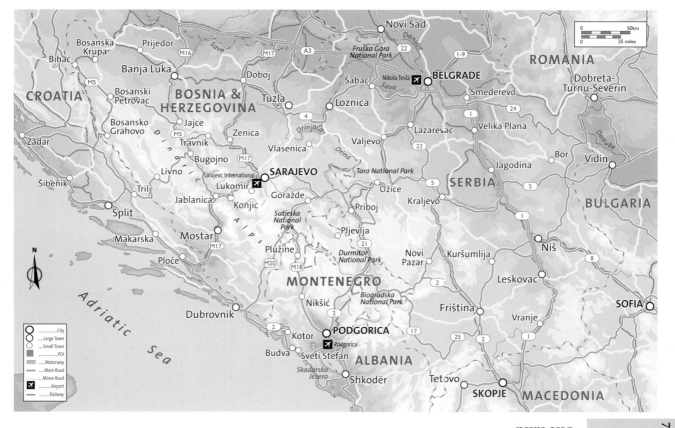

Serbia

Serbia proper shares borders to the north with Croatia, Hungary and Romania. The semi-autonomous province of Vojvodina, with its capital city Novi Sad, dominates the northern Pannonian plains. Serbia borders with Bulgaria to the east, Macedonia to the south, and Montenegro and Bosnia and Herzegovina to the west.

Serbia is dominated by the massive Pannonian and Danubian plains that extend from the north of the country deep into the central and southern regions. This area is the agricultural and industrial heart of Serbia. Its mountain ranges lie mainly along its borders. To the west and southwest are the country's highest mountains – the Dinaric Alps and Prokletija Mountains. To the east, Serbia shares a small portion of the Balkan Mountains with Bulgaria, and in the south the Sar Mountains (in Kosovo) create the southern frontier with Macedonia.

Serbia exclusively belongs to the Black Sea basin. It shares the Drina River with eastern Bosnia, which creates most of its western border. The navigable Sava River, which divides northern Bosnia and Croatia, flows into the Danube near Belgrade. The northeast of the country is part of the fertile Danubian plain and consists of the Tisa (Tisza) and Morava rivers – both tributaries to the Danube.

Agricultural fields of Vojvodina

Rijeka Crnojević (River Crnojević) town, Montenegro

Montenegro

Montenegro is part of the European middle Mediterranean region. It shares borders with Croatia and Bosnia and Herzegovina to the north, and its eastern frontier borders with both Serbia and Kosovo. The southern border is exclusively with Albania. The country is geographically divided into three regions: coastal, central and the northern mountains. Although all of Montenegro is extremely mountainous (its name means 'The Black Mountains'), it has two climate regions that create two distinct landscapes. The southern and central regions belong to the Adriatic Sea basin, and enjoy a sunny and mild Mediterranean climate. The northern regions just north of the capital Podgorica belong to the Black Sea basin and have a Continental Alpine climate zone. The entire country, however, is part of the Central Dinaric Alps mountain range that ends in the northern region by the town of Plav on the Albanian border. This range also dominates most of Bosnia and Herzegovina and large swathes of western Serbia. It is believed that it was due to this part of the mountain range that the invading Ottomans, who were able to conquer most of the Balkans in medieval times, never reached their cultural capital – Cetinje near the coast.

The coastal towns, the heart of Montenegrin tourism, are quite simply a magnificent mélange of the clear and tranquil Adriatic and the awe-inspiring mountains that tower from its shores.

History

BOSNIA AND HERZEGOVINA

1189   29 August – The Kulina Bana Charter trade agreement is signed between Bosnia and Dubrovnik.

1377   Bosnia becomes a kingdom under King Tvrtko I.

1463   The Ottomans conquer Bosnia.

1878   The Austro-Hungarian occupation of Bosnia and Herzegovina begins.

1908   5 October – Austria-Hungary annexes Bosnia and Herzegovina.

1914   28 June – Franz Ferdinand is assassinated by Gavrilo Princip sparking World War I.

1918   1 December – Bosnia and Herzegovina becomes part of the Kingdom of Serbs, Croats and Slovenes.

1939   26 August – Bosnia and Herzegovina is divided by the Croatian/Serbian agreement of Cvetkovic–Macek.

1941   6 April – Germany attacks and conquers Yugoslavia. 20 April – Bosnia and Herzegovina becomes a part of the Independent State of Croatia (NDH).

1943   25 November – Bosnia and Herzegovina's sovereignty restored at AVNOJ (the Anti-Fascist People's Council for Liberated Yugoslavia).

1945   29 November – Bosnia and Herzegovina becomes part of the new Yugoslavia.

1992   29 February – referendum for the independence of Bosnia and Herzegovina. 6 April – Bosnia and Herzegovina is recognised as an independent country; Bosnia and Herzegovina is attacked by the Yugoslav army.

1995   21 November – Dayton Peace Accords signed by Croatia, Bosnia and Herzegovina and Serbia/Montenegro.

2006   SFOR (Stabilisation Force) is transformed into a EUFOR (European

Union Force), a minimal European force, after Bosnia and Herzegovina celebrates a decade of peace implementation. Constitutional amendments needed for EU integration are narrowly rejected in parliament.

SERBIA

750 Founding of the first Serbian state after the collapse of East Roman rule.

1165 Serbia regains independence.

1346 Serbia becomes Kingdom of Serbia under the rule of Stefan Dusan.

1389 Historic defeat of Serbian forces against invading Turks.

1459 Ottomans exert control over all Serbian lands.

1815 Serbia gains some autonomy from Ottomans.

1828–9 Russo-Turkish war; Serbia granted rights as a principality within the Ottoman Empire but under the protection of Russia.

1878 Serbia totally freed from Ottoman occupation, and again becomes Kingdom of Serbia.

1918 After Austria is defeated in World War I, the Kingdom of Serbs, Croats and Slovenes is formed.

1934 King Alexander is assassinated.

1941 Yugoslavia is occupied by Italian and German forces.

1963 Reorganisation of Yugoslav into a federation of republics – Federal Socialist Republic of Yugoslavia (with much more self-management).

1989 Slobodan Milošević re-imposes direct rule over the autonomous provinces of Kosovo and Vojvodina.

1991 Slovenia and Croatia vote for independence.

1991–5 Milošević and the Serbian army war with Slovenia, Croatia and Bosnia and Herzegovina.

1995 The Dayton Peace Accords are signed with

History

Serbia, Croatia and Bosnia and Herzegovina.

1998 The Kosovo conflict begins to resurface.

1999 NATO bombs Serbia in response to the Kosovo crisis.

2000 Milošević is overthrown by popular protests.

2003 Pro-democratic president Zoran Djindic is assassinated in Belgrade by Serbian nationalist opposition.

2006 Talks for EU integration are halted due to a lack of cooperation with the International War Crimes Tribunal and because of not arresting war criminal General Ratko Mladic.

MONTENEGRO

15th–18th centuries Montenegro retains a substantial measure of autonomy from Ottoman Empire.

1798 Montenegro is acknowledged as an independent principality.

1878 Montenegrin independence is recognised under international treaties.

1918 Following World War I, Montenegro becomes part of the Kingdom of Serbs, Croats and Slovenes.

1929 Kingdom of Serbs, Croats and Slovenes is renamed Kingdom of Yugoslavia.

1945 After liberation, under Josip Broz Tito's leadership, the Federative People's Republic of Yugoslavia is formed.

1980 Tito dies.

1991 Milo Djukanovic becomes Montenegrin prime minister and supports Milošević.

1992 Montenegro joins Serbia in the Federal Republic of Yugoslavia.

1997 Djukanovic defeats the pro-Milošević candidate in the Montenegrin presidential election.

1999 Djukanovic declares Montenegro is neutral in the Kosovo conflict.

2002 January – Montenegro adopts the euro as its currency.
March – Montenegrin and Serbian leaders sign an accord to set up a new state called 'Serbia and Montenegro' replacing the rump of 'Yugoslavia'.
October – Parties allied with pro-independence Djukanovic win Montenegrin general elections. Djukanovic gives up the presidency to become coalition prime minister.

2003 January – Serbian and Montenegrin parliaments approve constitutional charter for the Union of Serbia and Montengro.

2004 May – Prominent journalist and critic of Montenegrin government, Dusko Jovanovic, is shot dead. His paper, *Dan*, is seen as a mouthpiece for the republic's anti-independence opposition.

2005 February – Montenegrin leaders suggest an early end to the Union of Serbia and Montenegro and the formation of two independent republics, which Serbia rejects.

2006 May – Montenegro holds an independence referendum. Just over the required 55 per cent of voters say yes.
June – Montenegro declares independence.
October–November – Prime Minister Milo Djukanovic steps down and is succeeded by his Democratic Party of Socialists ally, Zeljko Sturanovic.
December – NATO admits Montenegro to its Partnership for Peace pre-membership programme.

The flag of Belgrade

Politics

The collective political history of the western Balkan nations has shared a similar fate since the collapse of their medieval kingdoms in the 14th to 15th centuries to the invading Ottomans. From this point on, the politics of the Ottoman Empire, along with its struggles with Russia and Austria-Hungary, became the everyday political reality for the southern Slavs. It wasn't until the uprisings that began in Serbia in the early 1800s that Turkish control began to weaken. By 1878, the Ottoman Empire was in full retreat and a new tug-of-war for influence in the region began between the Russian and Austro-Hungarian empires. Foreign occupiers did not stop playing major political roles in the region until the assassination of Franz Ferdinand in Sarajevo in 1914, which sparked World War I.

The end of World War I marked the first time that the southern Slavs had full political control over their own destiny since the medieval era. The first Yugoslavia, formed in 1929, was wrought with poor economic conditions and struggled to appease the nationalist sentiments of the various Slav nations. It ended abruptly with the commencement of World War II, and most of the western Balkans came under Italian and/or German occupation. The partisan victory, led by Josip Broz Tito, gave birth to the second Yugoslavia. This Federative Socialist Republic created the longest and most harmonious era of Slav unity. After Tito's death in 1980, nationalist sentiment –

particularly from Serbia and Croatia – began to take centre stage in the political arena.

By 1991, Croatia and Slovenia had already declared independence from Yugoslavia. Bosnia and Herzegovina, stuck between the major conflict between Serbia and Croatia, also voted for independence but with a boycott from the Bosnian Serbs who made up 33 per cent of Bosnia and Herzegovina's population. President Milo Djukanovic of Montenegro first opted to side with Serbia and Slobodan Milošević to form a 'rump' Yugoslavia that went to war with Croatia and Bosnia and Herzegovina.

With the signing of the Dayton Peace Accords in 1995 came peace for

Bosnia and Herzegovina and Montenegro. Serbia, however, still dealing with the complicated Kosovo problem, soon found itself in yet another armed conflict with Kosovar Albanians and was eventually bombed by North Atlantic Treaty Organisation (NATO) forces. This created the first and what many consider the final rift between Montenegro and Serbia. The event led to a spirited independence campaign by Milošević's one-time Montenegrin ally Djukanovic. The EU managed to arbitrate a union of Serbia and Montenegro, which eventually failed and led to a referendum in 2006 in which just over the necessary 55 per cent of the voters in Montenegro voted for full independence.

This newly found 'independence' has brought about considerable change and, in some sense, growing pains. The wars and political instability that rocked this region in the 1990s have thankfully passed. Although nationalist parties still possess a tremendous amount of political clout, all three

countries have embarked on a new vision which means EU integration for the entire region. Despite the ever-present political turmoil and seemingly insurmountable corruption, all of these places will most likely seem 'normal' to the traveller, with no visible signs of their political woes.

Politics

MILO DJUKANOVIC

The former President and Prime Minister of Montenegro has a fascinating political background. He will certainly go down in the history books as the man who led Montenegro to independence. His political career, however, started when he became a loyal ally of Slobodan Milošević. Djukanovic played an active role in the war against Bosnia, swiftly apologising for any wrongdoings Montenegro may have been responsible for during the conflict. In the late 1990s he cut his ties with Milošević and soon began Montenegro's independence bid. Bowing to pressure by the EU not to hold a referendum in the early part of the 21st century, Djukanovic held out until 2006 when his independence campaign brought a 55 per cent 'yes' vote, creating the newest country in Europe.

Kalemegdan Fortress in Belgrade, where World War I began

Culture

Having been an integral part of Yugoslavia for almost half a century, all three republics certainly encompass a common cultural heritage. With the exception of Belgrade, and to a lesser extent Sarajevo and Novi Sad, the region is not known for its grandiose museums or ancient ruins. The collective cultural renaissance that took place in Tito's Yugoslavia is now being transformed, perhaps for the first time, under the premise of open and democratic societies. Despite, or maybe even because of, the dire political situation that defines the region, the creative industries of each nation are experiencing a new European renaissance. Belgrade and Sarajevo are producing some of Europe's finest films, hosting cutting-edge festivals and enjoying something that many in the West take for granted – cultural freedom.

The culture of the southern Slavs is a fascinating mix of East and West, Christianity and Islam, socialism and democracy. What many find to be most interesting and impressive about the culture of the region are the genuine hospitality, everyday traditions and customs, and the fine line between the old world and the new.

Bosnia and Herzegovina

Bosnia and Herzegovina is often referred to as 'little Yugoslavia'. The country has always been known for its multicultural composition, even after the war created many ethnic divides.

For this reason, it can be said that Bosnia and Herzegovina has one of the most diverse cultural heritages in the region. Islam and Orthodox Christianity from the East have met with the equally influential Austro-Hungarian and Catholic traditions from the West. Perhaps most fascinating to Westerners is the strong Oriental feel in the heart of Europe.

Bosnia and Herzegovina has long been known for its rich traditions in music and film. In Yugoslav times, during its cultural and social renaissance of the 1970s and 1980s, it always produced the best bands and music. The music scene is once again emerging as the region's best. Bosnia and Herzegovina's film industry has produced Oscar-winning productions, such as *No Man's Land* by Danis Tanovic, and the Berlin Golden Bear for best film was awarded to Jasmila Zbanic's *Grbavica*.

The post-war cultural revolution, which many consider to be ongoing, has seen Sarajevo emerge as a European capital city rather than a provincial one. Sarajevo's Film Festival, the Jazz Fest and its alternative theatre MESS festival have transformed into the best of their kind in the region – and each year they just seem to get better.

Serbia

Serbian culture seems to reinvent itself on a regular basis. Despite its successful and extremely talented creative industry, Serbian culture is most often portrayed through its long and tumultuous history. At times, it seems as if contemporary art is often dealt the back seat while ancient battles, songs and fairytales take centre stage. It is certainly true that Serbia has seen its fair share of wars, with empires sweeping through this key Balkan territory, and this has shaped the cultural heritage of the Serbs in a rather potent way.

What is not often mentioned about Serbian culture is the warm and friendly hospitality extended to complete strangers. The Serbs' love for music and dance, good wine and spirits, and many-day parties is very much a part of Serbian cultural lifestyles. The café culture so dominant in Bosnia is also found in Serbia.

Belgrade is the leader in former Yugoslavia in terms of the arts, with captivating theatre, film and orchestras.

Montenegro

Montenegro is by no means a bastion of cultural events and manifestations. This tiny nation does have, however, a long and rich cultural history. Montenegro's cultural heritage is similar to its natural one. The coastal cultures very much resemble the quaint settlements of any Mediterranean nation, with a plethora of folklore, superstition, and a knack for producing the country's finest artists. Most of the country's festivals take place during the summer months on the coast. The museums and impressive Mediterranean architecture are largely based along the Adriatic.

The crossroads of the Catholic and Orthodox influences are best represented in the monasteries in the Bay of Kotor. The Byzantine and Venetian empires both vied for power in Montenegro's coastal region and both left traces of their rich cultures. Earlier Illyrian, Greek and Roman cultures, which dominated the entire Balkan Peninsula, also left their footprints in both the coastal and highland areas. The northern territories are more rugged and traditional, and the cultural heritage is connected to the mountains and traditional lifestyles. Here, Orthodox Christian and a smaller Islamic influence meet in the remote highlands.

Festivals and events

Whatever the season, there is always an event to tempt most visitors. From the world-renowned Sarajevo Film Festival to more unusual celebrations such as the Guča Trumpet Festival, you'll be guaranteed a good time.

BOSNIA AND HERZEGOVINA

February/March

Sarajevan Winter A multi-faceted festival of artists from the former Yugoslavia and Europe.
Contact: Ibrahim Spahic, director, M. Tita 9a ili Gabelina 16. Tel: (033) 207 945/948. Fax: (033) 663 626. Email: ibrosa@bih.net.ba

July

Baščaršijske nights: Sarajevo For the entire month of July, the old town in Sarajevo hosts cultural events.
JU Sarajevo Art, Dalmatinska 2/1. Tel: (033) 207 921/929. Fax: (033) 207 972. Email: koncagsa@bih.net.ba. Free admission.

Mostar Summer Festival Mostar's summer festival hosts local productions in drama, music, art and film.

Una International Regatta: Bihac This rafting event is unmatched in the region and more and more enthusiasts gather to kayak, raft and have fun on Bosnia's most beautiful river. Late July.

August

Sarajevo Film Festival This has become one of the best film festivals in Europe.
Obala Art Centar, Hamdije Kreševljakovica 13. Tel: (033) 665 532, 668 186. Fax: (033) 664 547. Email: sff@sff.ba. www.sff.ba

October

MESS: Sarajevo Alternative and contemporary theatre and dance. Tickets can be purchased online.
M. Tita 54/1. Tel: (033) 200 392. Fax: (033) 211 972. Email: mess@mess.ba. www.mess.ba

November

Jazz festival: Sarajevo An intimate jazz experience with small venues.
Contact: Edin Zubcevic. Tel/Fax: (033) 659 692. Email: info@jazzfest.ba. www.jazzfest.ba

SERBIA
April
Days of Belgrade This festival celebrates Belgrade's anniversary as a city and its liberation from Turkish rule. *16–19 April. www.beograd.org.yu*

NOMUS: Novi Sad A classical music festival featuring the region's finest classical musicians and symphonies. *Katolička Porta 2/II. Tel: (021) 452 344. Email: mons@eunet.yu. www.nomus.org.yu*

June–October
100 days 100 events: Vrnjačka Banja Dedicated to promoting the cultural heritage of Serbia – the 100 events cover all forms of art. *30 June–15 October.*

July
EXIT Festival: Novi Sad The best of Europe's new and old bands, electronic and world music. *Pozorišni Trg 1. Tel: (021) 424 451. Fax: (021) 424 453. Email: office@exitfest.org. www.exitfest.org*

SARAJEVO FILM FESTIVAL

What started out as an act of creative resistance has turned into one of Europe's premiere film festivals. During the siege of Sarajevo, cultural life refused to bow to the endless siege; in 1995 a few young Sarajevans organised the first Sarajevo Film Festival, despite the city being under a blockade. Each year since, the festival has gained more and more of a reputation as a great venue for a regional and alternative film festival.

August
Belgrade Beer Fest The best of the region's beer in Kalemegdan Fortress. *16–20 August. www.belgradebeerfest.com*

Guča Trumpet Festival This brass band competition is an amazing taste of southern Serbia's brass brand traditions. *Early–mid-August. www.guca.co.yu*

Screenplay Festival: Vrnjačka Banja Focuses on the region's film industry. *www.screenfest.org.yu*

MONTENEGRO
February
Kotor Carnival Parade and masked ball. *www.kotorkarneval.com*

June
Mediterranean Song Festival: Budva A three-day local music festival.

July/August
Theatre City Festival: Budva An outdoor, rustic and grassroots festival of theatre, music, literature and arts. *1 July–20 August. www.gradteatar.cg.yu*

August
Herceg Novi's Film Festival This film festival offers some great local productions (with English subtitles). *Early August.*

September
International Festival of Alternative Theatre (FIAT): Podgorica Prestigious alternative theatre fest.

ROMANIA

CROATIA

Bosanska
Krupa
Bihać
Prijedor
Banja Luka
Doboj
Bosanska
Petrovac
Bosansko
Grahovo
Jajce
Travnik
Bugojno
Livno
Trilj
Jablanica
Konjic
Mostar
Makarska
Ploče
Zadar
Šibenik
Split

Sava
BOSNIA &
HERZEGOVINA
Tuzla
Zenica
Vlasenica
Drinjača
SARAJEVO
Lukomir
Goražde
Sutjeska
National
Park
Plužine
Durmitor
National Park
MONTENEGRO
Nikšić
Dubrovnik
Kotor
Budva
Sveti Stefan
Skadarsko
Jezero
Shkodër
Biogradska
National Park
PODGORICA

Novi Sad
Danube
Fruška Gora
National Park
Šabac
Sava
BELGRADE
Smederevo
Loznica
Lazarevac
Velika Plana
Valjevo
Drina
Tara National Park
Mokra
Gora
Užice
Kraljevo
Priboj
Pljevlja
Novi
Pazar
Kopaonik
2030
SERBIA
Jagodina
Bor
Vidin
Danube
BULGARIA
Niš
Kuršumlija
Leskovac
Priština
Vranje
SOFIA

ALBANIA
Tetovo
SKOPJE
MACEDONIA

Dobreta-
Turnu-Severin

Adriatic Sea

Dinaric Alps

N

Page	
26	Bosnia & Herzegovina
46	Serbia
68	Montenegro

Bosnia and Herzegovina

❶ Mostar's Stari Most (old bridge) The bridge that literally connected East with West spanned the Neretva River for over 400 years. It is Bosnia and Herzegovina's only UNESCO Cultural Heritage Site.

❷ Sarajevo's Baščaršija Possibly the most authentic taste of the Orient in the Balkans, Baščaršija in the old town resembles an Istanbul shopping and workshop quarter.

❸ Lukomir village The highest and most isolated mountain settlement in Bosnia and Herzegovina is literally a walk into medieval Europe. The highlanders here have preserved their traditional lifestyle in stunning surroundings.

❹ Sutjeska National Park This is one of the largest and oldest primeval forests in Europe. The protected Perucica Forest has some trees older than 500 years. The park is also home to Bosnia and Herzegovina's highest peak, Mount Maglic (2,386m/7,828ft).

Serbia

❺ Mokra Gora The old steam engine locomotives that used to travel from Belgrade to Sarajevo were put out of use in the 1970s. In the late 1990s, this old railway was reborn and today it is one of Serbia's most visited attractions.

❻ Fruška Gora National Park This interesting natural and monastic oasis pops up out of the flat Pannonian plains of northern Serbia. The area is home to 16 monasteries and as many beautiful country walks.

❼ Belgrade's old town A great taste of the former Yugoslavia's largest city. Belgrade is historically fascinating as well as having great café culture and nightlife.

Montenegro

❽ Bay of Kotor Europe's most southernmost fjord is a must-see for any visitors to Montenegro. The deep bay is surrounded by stunning limestone mountains.

❾ Durmitor National Park One of Europe's last patches of untouched wilderness. The park includes the Tara River Canyon, the deepest in Europe at 1,300m (4,265ft).

❿ Sveti Stefan If there's a glamorous side to Montenegro, Sveti Stefan would have to be it. The island has received a long list of famous guests who choose to make this their holiday spot.

⓫ Skadarsko Jezero (Lake Skadar) This is one of Europe's largest natural lakes, with the country's largest bird migration sanctuary.

Suggested itineraries

The seven-day tours outlined here are meant to be a general guide to a few of the many options you have when travelling in the region. These itineraries can be combined to visit two or more countries, depending on your schedule and the amount of travelling you would like to do. These are tested routes that prove feasible when taking into consideration distance, access and variation of attractions.

ONE WEEK
Bosnia and Herzegovina

Day 1 Arrive in Sarajevo, and tour Sarajevo city. See Baščaršija, the oriental quarter of Sarajevo's old town.

Day 2 Visit Lukomir and take a walk in the highest and most isolated mountain village in Bosnia.

Day 3 Take a boat ride on Vodeni Ciro in Drina Canyon. The new boat ride takes you through the gorgeous canyon of the Drina River.

Day 4 Day trip to Kraljeva Sutjeska and Franciscan Monastery. This quaint town was once the royal residence of the last Bosnian queen.

Day 5 Rafting on Neretva: II class. Fun and easy rafting on the crystal-clear Neretva River near Konjic.

Day 6 Mostar – city tour and see the UNESCO old bridge (Stari Most). Mostar is the country's most beautiful city.

Day 7 Visit Počitelj and Blagaj; return to Sarajevo. Počitelj and Blagaj are tiny Ottoman settlements just south of Mostar.

Day 8 Departure.

Serbia

Day 1 Arrive in Belgrade. Tour the city and visit the Kalemegdan complex. Check out Belgrade's fun and exciting atmosphere.

Day 2 Visit Ada recreation centre. Take a day and relax by the lake or at the bohemian cafés.

Day 3 Travel to Novi Sad. Explore the city and visit Petrovaradin Fortress. This city claims to be the Serbian Athens for its rich cultural heritage.

Day 4 Day trip to Fruška Gora. A great walking area and an opportunity to see a few of the park's 16 monasteries.

Day 5 Travel to Zlatibor – spend the afternoon in the Zlatibor region. Enjoy Serbia's most popular nature getaway.

Day 6 Visit Mokra Gora village and take a train ride. An old-style village with a steam engine locomotive ride to match.

Day 7 Tara National Park. Visit the beautiful park and take a boat ride through the wonderful canyons of the Drina River.

Day 8 Departure from Belgrade.

Montenegro

Day 1 Arrive in Dubrovnik and transfer to Kotor. Tour the city of Kotor – see the old town and enjoy its energy.

Day 2 Bay of Kotor: two islands and Prerast. Take a day-long boat trip to the two islands and have lunch in Prerast village.

Day 3 Budva Riveria – Budva old town. Visit Montenegro's oldest coastal city and beautiful old town.

Day 4 Sveti Stefan. Take a day to wander along the high street and enjoy the beaches and glamour.

Day 5 Cetinje – visit the town and walk to Njegoš' Mausoleum. See Montenegro's historical capital and the mausoleum in beautiful Lovćen National Park.

Day 6 Visit Skadarsko Jezero (Lake Skadar), take a boat ride on the lake, and stay overnight in Ulcinj. One of Europe's largest and most beautiful lakes on the border with Albania.

Day 7 Spend the day at Ada Bojana's sandy beaches and relax in the sun or try out the watersports.

Day 8 Departure.

Suggested itineraries

The enormous Kalemegdan complex is not to be missed

TWO-WEEK COMBINATION TRIPS

All three of the following itineraries make a full circle from place of arrival to departure. The trips are only suggestions and include a range of activities, from cultural city tours through walking in nature to boat rides, and chilling out on the beach. Many adjustments and/or modifications can be made to suit your travels.

Montenegro and Bosnia and Herzegovina

Day 1 Fly into Dubrovnik. Stay overnight.

Day 2 Travel to Kotor and visit the city. Stay overnight.

Day 3 Visit Kotor Bay; take the island monastery trip. Stay overnight in Kotor.

Day 4 Travel to Budva and visit Sveti Stefan. Stay overnight in Budva.

Day 5 Go to the Ada Bojana beaches. Stay overnight in Ulcinj.

Day 6 Travel to Durmitor National Park; stop over at Cetinje on the way. Stay overnight in Zabljak.

Day 7 Enjoy a day's walk in Durmitor. Stay overnight in Zabljak.

Day 8 Travel to Sarajevo and explore the city. Stay overnight.

Day 9 Spend the day in Sarajevo's old oriental town, Baščaršija. Stay overnight.

Day 10 Take a day trip to Kraljeva Sutjeska Franciscan Monastery and enjoy the hill walk. Stay overnight in Sarajevo.

Day 11 Day trip: rafting on Neretva River, class II. Stay overnight in Mostar.

Day 12 City tour of Mostar and visit the old bridge (Stari Most). Stay overnight.

Day 13 Visit Kravica Waterfalls and lunch at the Mogorjelo Roman ruins. Visit the Vjetrenica Caves near Ravno in Popovo Polje. Travel to and stay overnight in Dubrovnik.

Day 14 Departure from Dubrovnik.

Dubrovnik, Montenegro, and Bosnia and Herzegovina

Day 1 Fly into Dubrovnik. Stay overnight.

Day 2 Spend the day in Dubrovnik and visit Lokrum Island. Stay overnight in Dubrovnik.

Day 3 Travel to Kotor and visit the old town. Stay overnight.

Day 4 Go on the Bay of Kotor island boat ride. Stay overnight in Kotor.

Day 5 Visit Budva and Sveti Stefan. Stay overnight in Budva.

Day 6 See Ada and Skadar lakes. Stay overnight in Ulcinj.

Day 7 Visit Cetinje and travel on to Durmitor National Park. Stay overnight in Zabljak.

Day 8 Day trip to Durmitor. Stay overnight in Zabljak.

Day 9 Travel to Sarajevo and explore the city. Stay overnight.

Day 10 Day trip to Lukomir, Bosnia's medieval village. Stay overnight in Sarajevo.

Day 11 Travel to Mostar, see the city and visit the old bridge (Stari Most). Stay overnight.

Day 12 From Mostar, visit Blagaj and Počitelj Ottoman settlements. Stay overnight in Mostar.

Day 13 Travel from Mostar to Dubrovnik, visiting the Vetrjenica Caves and lunching in Trebinje. Stay overnight in Dubrovnik.

Day 14 Morning shopping, departure from Dubrovnik.

Montenegro, Bosnia and Herzegovina, and Serbia

Day 1 Fly into Sarajevo. Stay overnight.

Day 2 Spend the day in Sarajevo touring the city's old town and centre. Stay overnight.

Day 3 Day trip to Lukomir village. Stay overnight in Sarajevo.

Day 4 Travel to Novi Sad (by bus) and explore the city. Stay overnight.

Day 5 Fruška Gora National Park – walk, monastery and vineyards tour. Stay overnight in Novi Sad.

Day 6 Travel to Belgrade and visit Belgrade's old town. Stay overnight.

Day 7 Spend the day in Belgrade and Ada Ciglanjin. Stay overnight in Belgrade.

Day 8 Take a train ride to Podgorica. Stay overnight.

Day 9 Travel to Budva and visit the old town and Sveti Stefan. Stay overnight in Budva.

Day 10 Travel to Kotor and spend the day in Kotor's old town. Stay overnight.

Day 11 Visit Kotor Bay and take the monastery islands boat ride. Stay overnight in Kotor.

Day 12 Travel to Mostar via Trebinje (have lunch and go for a stroll in Trebinje). Stay overnight in Mostar.

Day 13 Tour Mostar city, visit Blagaj (have lunch here) and return to Sarajevo. Stay overnight in Sarajevo.

Day 14 Morning shopping and relax, departure from Sarajevo.

View of Novi Sad across the Danube

Bosnia and Herzegovina

Bosnia and Herzegovina are two regions on each side of the towering Dinaric Alps, where a mild Mediterranean climate and a harsher continental climate converge. Herzegovina has always had a cultural history distinct from Bosnia, although there are many similarities in language, ethnicity, culture and identity.

BOSNIA
Sarajevo

Walking through Sarajevo is the equivalent of walking along a historical timeline. The quaint old Turkish quarter of Baščaršija built in the 15th and 16th centuries has retained its authentic characteristics as a buzzing oriental trading centre. The Austro-Hungarian era city centre very much resembles old Vienna, with its trademark architecture and superb urban spacing. This was followed by the occasionally daunting socialist architecture of Tito's era, when the city expanded fivefold in as many decades.

Sarajevo is not a city of majestic museums or perfectly preserved medieval castles. It is a fun and vital city with a café culture unmatched anywhere in Europe. It has been called the fastest-changing city in Europe.

The reasons for this are fairly obvious as the city was brought to its knees during the longest siege in modern European history from 1992–5, but it has now re-emerged. In fact, it has transformed from a provincial capital to a bustling and exciting European capital city.

Old town and city centre

The old town of Sarajevo was largely built during the 400 years of Ottoman dominance in this region. Many of the quarters are markedly oriental, particularly the trading centre of Baščaršija, which is the heart of the tourism attractions in the city. The old town has maintained much of its ancient flavour with the preservation of *stari zanati*, the old crafts that have been practised by craftspeople on the same streets for centuries.

Bosnia and Herzegovina

Sarajevo's old town

With the exception of a few sights high up on the surrounding hills, the old town is walkable, and Sarajevo is the perfect city for easy wanders with the old town being by far the most fascinating part.

Although closely linked with the old town, the city centre is the political and administrative hub of Sarajevo. It was built at the beginning of the 20th century when Bosnia and Herzegovina was part of the Austro-Hungarian Empire. The architecture and urban layout differs from that of the old Turkish era quarters, and the city centre has a distinct Viennese feel to it. This area was heavily damaged during the war in the 1990s, but it has recently had a facelift with new façades of many colours, pavements and asphalted roads.

As a natural extension from the old town, the sights and attractions in the city centre are compact and easy to access by foot. The Ferhadija walkway eventually merges with Titova Street near the Vječna Vatra (Eternal Flame), and this is a good reference point when strolling – from here you will easily find your way back towards the old town. Parallel to Titova Street to the south is the Miljacka River. It runs in a clear east–west direction in the valley, acting as the best orientation landmark in town.

The heart of the old town is Baščaršija. **Sebilj Fountain**, or Pigeon Square as some call it, is where the main public fountain is located and this is your best focal point when wandering in the old town. The coffee and sweet shops near Sebilj Fountain

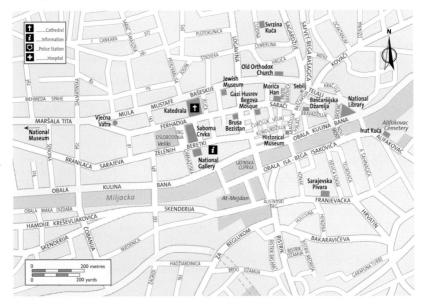

The Vijećnica (National Library) was originally the town hall in Sarajevo

all serve Turkish coffee with Turkish delight, called *rahatlokum* in Bosnian.

Just outside the square is **Kazandžiluk Street**, the famous coppersmith trading place on the east side of Baščaršija. Here you'll find great antiques, hand-carved copper dishes and oriental décor.

Next to Kazandžiluk Street is **Baščaršija Džamija**, or the Marketplace Mosque. Its official name is Džamija Havadže Duraka (Havadja Durak's Mosque) and it was built in the 1530s. This mosque often has the imam (local Muslim priest) sing the call to prayer from the minaret. Its mystical sounds resonate throughout the *čaršija*.

On Bravadziluk, where all the sumptuous eating places are, is the **Vijećnica** (National Library), built during Austrian rule in Bosnia and Herzegovina. Originally used as the town hall during the Habsburg rule, it was converted to the library after their abrupt departure. Centuries of history went up in flames when Serbian forces deliberately targeted the building with incendiary grenades in the early days of the siege in the 1990s. Everything was lost. The building is still under reconstruction, but on completion it will once again be one of the most beautiful buildings in the entire country.

Across the river from Vijećnica is the **Inat Kuća** (*Veliki Alifakovac 1; tel: (033) 447 867*) – one of the most famous traditional restaurants in town. Passing Inat Kuća to the right is **Alifakovac Street**. Alifakovac is the eastern quarter of old Sarajevo and is dominated by a beautiful and very old Muslim cemetery. The Alifakovac graveyard was a final resting place for

Muslim foreigners who died and were buried in Sarajevo. The cemetery is interesting from a historical viewpoint and also for the great views of the old town that it offers.

Ferhadija walkway is perhaps the most charming part of town. It stretches from Sebilj in the heart of Baščaršija all the way to the Vječna Vatra (Eternal Flame) in the city centre. The area is almost always filled with locals strolling through town, window-shopping, chatting or just enjoying walking up and down. Along the Ferhadija walkway, still in Baščaršija, is **Morića Han** (*Sarači 77; open: daily 7am–10pm*). The function of the *han* was to provide warehouse space, stables and accommodation for traders coming from Asia Minor and Dubrovnik. The courtyard is a lovely place to sit and have a drink. There is also a Persian rug centre here owned by a very knowledgeable Iranian professor.

The Saborna Crkva in Trg Oslobođenja

Begova Džamija (Gazi Husrev Bey's Mosque) on Ferhadija, a very short distance from Morića Han, is the most significant Islamic symbol in Bosnia and Herzegovina. It is perhaps the finest example of Ottoman Islamic architecture on the Balkan Peninsula. Open to visitors at certain times of the day, it is important to stay to the side during prayer time. This is the main mosque in the city and is usually filled with local worshippers.

At the end of the marble-like walkway in the old quarter is the **Brusa Bezistan** (*Abadžiluk 10; open: Mon–Fri 8am–8pm, Sat 9am–2pm; closed: Sun*). This beautiful oriental department store, with a long corridor topped by six domes, was the main trading centre for silk from Bursa in Asia Minor and is definitely worth a browse.

Sarajevo is a city of many beautiful Ottoman bridges, the most famous being the **Latinska Ćuprija**, which is also still referred to as Principov Most (Princip's Bridge). It was here that Archduke Ferdinand and his pregnant wife were shot and killed on 28 June 1914 (St Vitus' Day) by Gavrilo Princip. It is believed that this act was the catalyst for World War I. By crossing the Latinska Ćuprija, you enter the **Bistrik** district of the old town. The park along the river is a favourite gathering spot during the summer. Called At-Mejdan, this area is a tree-covered green space that provides a cool and pleasant break from the hot summer days and a nice place for children to play.

Around the corner from At-Mejdan on Franjevacki Street is the **Sarajevska Pivara** (Brewery) (*Franjevačka 15*). The brewery played a great role in the survival of the city during the siege. It is built on top of one of the largest freshwater springs in the city. With all water cut off, this became the only source of clean drinking water for thousands of Sarajevans. The brewery has recently opened a new *pivnica* (brewery bar and restaurant) that serves the only dark beer made in Sarajevo on tap. The beer is good and there is a great atmosphere in the evenings.

To see an authentic Ottoman house from the 18th century, pay a visit to the **Svrzina Kuća** (Svrzo's House, *Glodžina 8, parallel with Logavina Street; tel: (033) 535 264; www.muzejsarajevo.ba; open: Tue–Sat 10am–5pm, Sun 10am–1pm; closed: Mon; admission charge*). This house/museum is a great example of a wealthy *beg*'s (leader) house. The high walls around the garden mark the intimate and secret life of the wealthier *begs*. The balconies are made of intricately carved wood and the large sitting rooms are typical of Ottoman homes that were created to receive a large extended family. The house has been restored and guided tours through the house are possible throughout the week.

Back on Ferhadija Street in the city centre is the main landmark, the **Katedrala** (Cathedral, *open: daily 8.30am–4pm*). This was completed in 1889 when the Austrians had gained full control of the city. The cathedral is usually open for visitors. Don't be surprised to find Sarajevo's youth hanging out on the steps of the cathedral; it has always been a popular (and central) place to meet friends.

Following Ferhadija to **Trg Oslobođenja** (Liberation Square), you come across the **Saborna Crkva**. This is

Latinska Ćuprija

the largest Orthodox church in Sarajevo. It is open to visitors most days. The square is also home to a consistent group of pensioners who play chess here, rain or shine. Directly across the street from the square is the **Nacionalna galerija Bitt–Umjetnička galerija** (National Gallery of Bosnia and Herzegovina, *Zelenih Beretki 8. Open: 10am–3pm. Admission charge*). In this gallery the works of the best artists of Bosnia and Herzegovina, past and present, are displayed.

As Ferhadija meets Tito Street, the **Vječna Vatra** (Eternal Flame) burns in memory of the Serbs, Croats, Muslims and other partisans who gave their lives in the liberation of Sarajevo from the fascists in World War II. From here, the main thoroughfare of Tito's Street opens up with brand-name shops,

restaurants, and at least half a dozen cafés.

Gradski Muzej Brusa Bezistan (City Museum Brusa Bezistan)

This relatively new museum was completed in 2004. It is situated right in the centre of town, in a beautiful six-dome Ottoman building. The collection – costumes, coins, tombstones and other items – is tastefully exhibited and accompanied by interesting texts in excellent English.
Brusa Bezistan, Kundurdžiluk 10. Tel: (033) 239 590. Open: Tue–Sat 10am–5pm, Sun 10am–1pm. Closed: Mon. Admission charge.

Historijski Muzej (Historical Museum)

The Historical Museum is located in a much smaller socialist-era building just 50m (55yds) west of Zemaljski muzej

Zemaljski Muzej (National Museum)

TETKA

During any war or great historical event we often read about the actions of leaders and politicians, but very rarely hear about the ordinary people who do extraordinary things during the most trying times. Tetka from Sarajevo is one of those people. *Tetka* means 'auntie' in the local language – she got the name after setting up a soup kitchen during the war to feed the elderly and disadvantaged. The end of the war brought about many changes but for the needy, times didn't get much better. So Tetka, now well into her 60s, continues to this day to feed her fellow Sarajevans from her tiny kitchen in Bistrik, with help and donations from those more fortunate.

(National Museum). The exhibition on the recent war is impressive simply due to the fact that it is a fresh topic, but otherwise it lacks style, variety and content.

Zmaja od Bosne 5. Tel: (033) 210 418. Fax: (033) 210 416. Email: histmuz@bih.net.ba. Open: Tue–Fri 9am–2pm, Sat & Sun 9am–1pm. Closed: Mon. Admission charge.

Stara Ortodoksna Crkva i Muzej (Old Orthodox Church and Museum)

Located in the heart of the old town, this house of worship is best known for its very large iconostasis that covers the entire right wall. The accompanying museum is well lit and has a more modern feel to it. It features Bibles, paintings, frescoes, ceremonial ornaments and a few gowns, all from the period between the 15th and 18th centuries.

Mula Mustafe Bešeskije 59. Tel: (033) 571 760. Museum open: Tue–Sun 10am–3pm. Closed: Mon & Orthodox holidays. Church open: Mon–Sun 8am–5pm. Admission charge.

Zemaljski Muzej (National Museum)

This museum, like most other things in Sarajevo, came out of the war in the 1990s looking battered. However, its exterior has been renovated beautifully – so much so, that the museum entrance pales in comparison. By far the most interesting item is exhibited in the small room on the first floor: the *Sarajevo Haggadah*. This 14th-century Spanish-Jewish book portrays the world as being round –

The Vječna Vatra (Eternal Flame) is dedicated to the partisan liberators of Sarajevo

unheard of at that time. In the centre courtyard there is the botanical garden with its *stećci* (medieval tombstones). The ethnographic exhibition on display in the building on the left is the only part of the museum with good English-language explanations.
Zmaja od Bosne 3. Tel: (033) 668 025, 668 026. Fax: (033) 262 710. Email: z.muzej@zemaljskimuzej.ba. www.zemaljskimuzej.ba. Open: Tue–Fri 10am–2pm, Sun 10am–2pm. Closed: Mon & Sat. Admission charge.

Židovski Muzej (Jewish Museum)

When the Jews were expelled from Spain in the late 15th century, it was the Ottoman Empire that welcomed them and placed them throughout their empire. The arrival, lifestyle and treatment of the Jews that settled in and around Sarajevo are told through this museum. The descriptions are in good English and the material is exhibited tastefully.
Velika Avlija bb. Tel: (033) 533 431. Fax: (033) 215 532. Open: Mon–Sun 10am–5pm. Admission charge.

DAY TRIPS FROM SARAJEVO
Ilidža and Vrelo Bosne

Ilidža is the western suburb of Sarajevo. It is easily reached by tram, bus or taxi from the city. The sights in Ilidža are largely nature based. The greatest attraction is the peace and quiet of Vrelo Bosne Park, which has lovely walking paths, a plethora of freshwater springs and the healing waters of its thermal spas. For the skier, Ilidža is just a 20-minute drive from the slopes of Bjelašnica.

Vrelo Bosne Park

The park has acres of lush green fields, a large picnic and playing area for children, and two traditional restaurants near one of the largest waterfalls in the park. It's an ideal way to beat the heat, but be aware that at weekends the park is extremely crowded. The springs are accessible by car, foot, bike or horse and carriage from the long, tree-lined *aleja* (walkway) that starts behind Hotel Terme and extends all the way into the park.

Vrelo Bosne Park

Terme Ilidža

This modern swimming complex was completed in 2006 and consists of large indoor and outdoor swimming pools that operate all year round. There are also a café and restaurant, changing room, jacuzzi and facilities for children, making it an ideal place for a day trip or a rainy day.

Mala Aleja 40 (behind Dom Zdravlje). Tel: (033) 771 011. Fax: (033) 771 010. Email: info@terme-catez.si. www.terme-ilidza.ba. Swimming pool open: 9am–9pm. Admission charge. Tropical garden open: 8am–10pm. Restaurant open: 8.30am–10.30pm.

Vodeni Ciro

This is a new and exciting boat cruise through the stunning Drina Canyon in eastern Bosnia. Just 90 minutes from Sarajevo, the Aquatic Choo-choo travels the same route as the old steam engine train from Sarajevo to Belgrade. This all-day cruise takes you through amazing untouched canyon lands.

Green Visions. Tel: (033) 717 290. Email: sarajevo@greenvisions.ba. www.greenvisions.ba

Kraljeva Sutjeska and Bobovac
Kraljeva Sutjeska

This charming and exceptionally well-kept village is only an hour's drive from Sarajevo. The Franciscan church and monastery has been the centre of life in this settlement since the Middle Ages. Kraljeva Sutjeska and the citadel at Bobovac were once the seat of two Bosnian kings, Tomač and Tvrtko of the Kotromanić dynasty. The last Bosnian queen, St Katarina, is still mourned today by the local townswomen, who wear black scarves as part of the traditional dress. It hosts two quaint but rather interesting museums, one a

Bobovac Mausoleum in Kraljeva Sutjeska

Visoko Pyramids

Despite the claims of some sceptics, the Bosnian Pyramid mystery has turned into the largest archaeological dig site in Europe. With confirmation from many world experts and several of Egypt's leading pyramidologists, the possibility of the Visoko Pyramids becoming a reality seems more likely every day. There is much more work to be done, but it has been confirmed that what has been uncovered is certainly manmade, prehistoric and colossal.

Excavations around Visočica

Attending a cultural exhibition in Sarajevo several years ago, Semir Osmanagic met a professor from Visoko. The two started talking about Osmanagic's interest in pyramids and the professor proclaimed, 'You want pyramids, come to Visoko and see this!' Osmanagic took the professor up on his offer and in April 2005, during a visit to Visoko, Osmanagic noticed two geometrically symmetrical elevations: Visočica Hill (now called the Bosnian pyramid of Sun) and Plješevica Hill (now called the Bosnian pyramid of Moon). Even though there was significant tree cover on the hills, it was evident that both of them shared characteristics of pyramids. The shapes and angles that Osmanagic had studied in Central and South America, Egypt and now here gave him reason to believe that he was looking at pyramids.

Although many were cynical, Osmanagic had no doubt that he had ventured upon what he describes as the greatest discovery in modern European history. After visiting the site, scepticism seems to quickly fade. The large hand-carved platforms, the symmetrically dug tunnels and the wide stone paths clearly indicate a massive manmade structure. The hills

View from beneath Visočica Hill

do resemble perfect pyramid shapes, and the more excavations that are completed, the more convincing Osmanagic's arguments seem to be. There is geological sedimentary verification that Visočica Hill is a massive stone object in the shape of a pyramid. Excavations have uncovered large slabs of hand-carved stone at every level of the hill. Plješevica Hill shows perfectly identical dimensions on satellite, radar and thermal images – proving the structure is of an artificial nature.

The results of anthropological genetics testing have proved that Bosnia and the Adriatic pool is the second-oldest oasis of life in Europe, with an estimated 27,000 years of uninterrupted human life. Part of Osmanagic's theory is that this part of the Balkans was an oasis for human settlements during the last ice age, almost 10,000 years ago. Here, and in several other places in Europe, human civilisation managed to survive in what was called a 'green belt'. Research lends itself to the theory that the pyramids were at one time under water, which, according to Osmanagic and his team, would place the age of the pyramids at over 10,000 years. Osmanagic argues that the submersion could only be attributed to melting ice. Many experts who agree with the theory are still not convinced of the pyramids' age, but more and more are starting to ponder the possibilities that Bosnia is one of Europe's oldest civilisations. The pyramids can be visited and viewed on site, and there is a good chance of meeting Osmanagic himself if he's not too busy digging.

library and the other an exhibition hall (*Tel: (032) 779 015/291. Open: By request & on Wed, Fri & Sat. Free admission, but there is a donation box in the museum*). The Dusper House in the village is the oldest house in central Bosnia, dating back to the early 18th century. The house has been designated a protected national monument and is open to visitors.

Bobovac Fortress

The fortress is strategically situated on a high ridge above the Bukovica Stream, some 5km (3 miles) from Kraljeva Sutjeska. Initially, the inhabitants of Kraljeva Sutjeska sought shelter here when they were under attack. In the dangerous years before the final invasion by the Ottomans, they

moved here permanently. Bobovac is not accessible by car. To get there, it is a pleasant one-hour walk from Kraljeva Sutjeska along the Bukovica Stream and through thick beech tree forests.

Travnik

Travnik is a 90-minute trip west from Sarajevo, reached by several daily buses or by car if you have one. This is the birthplace of Ivo Andrić, winner of the Nobel Laureate for Literature, and author of *Bridge on the Drina*. He also wrote *Travnik Chronicles*, which portrayed his view of life in Travnik during Ottoman rule. The Ivo Andrić House is now a museum and a restaurant (*Rodna Kuća Ive Andrića, Zenjak 9; www.nobelovac.travnik.ba. Open: Mon–Fri 8am–3pm, Sat & Sun*

The River Lašva runs through Travnik

10am–2pm. Admission charge). The museum's curator and Ivo Andrić enthusiast is Enes Skrgo. He speaks good English and is a great city guide. His knowledge of details and history add a great deal to the Travnik experience.

Another must-see in Travnik is the recently renovated medieval fortress (*Stari Grad Kastel, Varoš bb. Admission charge*) that dominates the skyline, and from which there are good views of the town. There are now regular opening hours and exhibitions as well as local women selling their handicrafts in the summer months.

You'd be ill-advised to ignore a visit Plava Voda (Blue Waters), a large spring that flows from the base of Vlašić Mountain. Although the source is known as Plava Voda, it is more famous for its outdoor eatery square. There are restaurants situated just below the source that prepare *ćevapi* (small meat sausage) and other traditional meals.

It's hard to miss the Šarena Džamija (Multi-coloured Mosque), built in 1757. With its bright colours, unique and intricate artistic details on the outside walls and carved wood, it is said to be among the most beautiful mosques in the Balkans.

HERZEGOVINA
Mostar old town

The old Turkish town has always been the main attraction in Mostar. Even though it took a beating from the

IVO ANDRIĆ (1892–1975)

Yugoslavia's only Nobel prize winner has a rather confusing background. Ivo Andrić's Nobel Laureate for Literature was awarded to him for his novel *Cuprija na Drina* (Bridge on the Drina). Andrić was born in Travnik, to a Croatian family. He left for Visegrad, where he found the inspiration for his novel. In essence, he's a Bosnian Croat – yet Serbia, and Bosnia and Herzegovina, both claim him as 'one of theirs'. Regardless of who claims him, Andrić was not only a great writer but a humble citizen of Yugoslavia. He donated all of his prize money to building libraries throughout Bosnia and Herzegovina and lived out his life in Belgrade.

conflict in the early 1990s, the city has made a tremendous comeback and is certainly in the running for the most beautiful city in Bosnia and Herzegovina. The old town is very compact and ideal for a walking tour – most of the main tourist sights can be seen in one day. The old town is enticing, particularly along the Neretva River, which can often lead to sitting for hours, just soaking up the sights and sounds. Unlike most tourist places, café and restaurant owners will never ask you to leave even if you've been sipping a Turkish coffee for two hours.

Bišćevića Kuća (Bišćevića House)

This is a 17th-century Turkish house located on the eastern banks of the Neretva River. There is a conversation or gathering room (*divanhan*) preserved in authentic Turkish style. Throughout the house are original household objects, and the courtyard is a fine example of the Ottoman style. *Bišćevića ulica. Admission charge.*

Kajtazova Kuća (Kajtaz House)

A bit off the centre circuit of the old town, this is the best-preserved Turkish-style house in Herzegovina. The Kajtaz House has been named a UNESCO World Heritage Site and is now protected by law as the finest example of an Ottoman home. The elderly owners are extremely friendly and make the best rose petal juice in Herzegovina.
Gase Ilića 21. Tel: (036) 550 913.

Stari Most in Mostar

Karadjozbegova Džamija (Karadjoz Beg Mosque)

This is the most important and significant example of sacred Islamic architecture in all of Herzegovina. Completed in 1557, its designer was Kodža Mimara Sinan, a great Turkish architect. The interior, Ottoman in style, has lost much of its detailed paintings through water damage.
Ulica braće Fejića. Admission charge.

Koski Mehmed-pašina Džamija (Koski Mehmeđ-Pasha Mosque)

Built in 1617, this mosque is open to visitors who may enter it and take photos for a small fee. Although it isn't always required, it is customary to remove shoes before entering. Women do not need to cover themselves as this mosque was especially designated to show Mostar's many guests the beauty of Ottoman Islamic architecture. For those willing to brave the dizzy spiral to the top, the minaret is also open to the public and is accessible from inside the mosque. The view speaks for itself!
Tepa.

Kriva Cuprija (Sloping Bridge)

The oldest single-arch stone bridge in Mostar is the Kriva Ćuprija over the Radobolje River, built in 1558 by the Turkish architect Cejvan Kethoda. It is believed to have been a test run for the construction of the Stari Most (Old Bridge) several years later. From here, quaint souvenir shops and galleries line the narrow streets of the old town as you near the old bridge.

on the tradition of *stari zanati* (old crafts) from father to son.

Kujundžiluk (Old Bazaar)

This area was named after the goldsmiths who traditionally created and sold their wares on this street. It is the best place in town to find authentic paintings and copper or bronze carvings of the Stari Most (Old Bridge), pomegranates (the national symbol of Herzegovina) or the famed *stećaks* (medieval tombstones). Carpet-makers, coppersmiths and antique collectors all continue to pass

Muzej Hercegovine (Museum of Herzegovina)

As well as being open to visitors, this museum gives researchers and students access to archives and documentary files (including films). It was founded in 1950 to promote the archaeological, ethnographic, literary and cultural history of Herzegovina. *Bajatova 4. Tel/fax: (036) 551 602. Open: Mon–Fri 9am–2pm, Sat 10am–noon.*

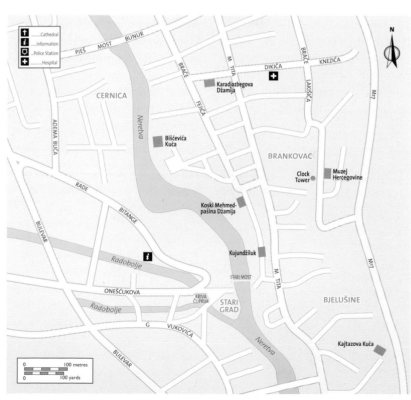

Walk: Blagaj

Blagaj's old town has recently developed a cultural heritage trail, which is certainly worthwhile for a relaxing stroll.

The trail around the town is a rather pleasant 30- to 45-minute walk starting at the Tekija Dervish House. A relatively easy trek to the Herceg Stjepan Fortress above Blagaj would add another 90 minutes to your trip.

To get to Blagaj, take bus No 10 from the Mostar central station.

1 Tekija Dervish House

The Tekija was built in the 1500s for the dervish cults at the base of a 200m (656ft) cliff wall. It is open to visitors all year round and serves cold drinks, Turkish tea and coffee in a beautiful garden overlooking the Buna River source. Entrance to the garden is free but there is an admission charge to enter the house.

Follow the trail to Velagić.

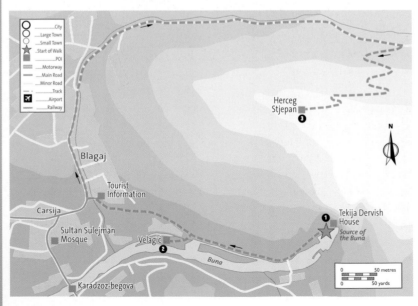

Tekija Dervish House in Blagaj

2 Velagić

The next official stop on the
heritage trail after the Dervish
House is the famous Velagić
Ottoman complex which was
built in the 17th century.

*The trail then leads towards town to the
old carsija (trading centre), and then to
the Sultan Sulejman Mosque (dating
from 1520) and the beautiful Ottoman
bridge Karadzoz-begova, which was
built in 1570. The well-kept paved trail*
*then follows the Buna River back to its
source on the other side.*

3 Herceg Stjepan

Atop the high cliffs is the fortress of
Herceg Stjepan. The fort is accessible
by a winding trail that takes about
45 minutes to walk. Although the trail
is marked in some places, it is not in
others, but it is generally easy to find.
There are no entrance fees to the fort,
and the views are spectacular.

Stari Most (Old Bridge)

No matter how many times you do it, crossing the Stari Most always seems to be an exciting experience. This single-arch stone bridge is an exact replica of the original bridge that stood for over 400 years and was designed by Hajrudin, a student of the great Turkish architect Sinan. It spans 28.7m (94ft) of the Neretva River, 21m (69ft) above the summer water level.

DAY TRIP FROM MOSTAR
Počitelj

This is a perfect half-day trip from Mostar or a stop-over on your way to the coast. A visit to this ancient Ottoman settlement can also be combined with a trip to Hutovo Blato Bird Reserve or Kravica Waterfalls near Ljubuski (*see pp93 & 101*).

Počitelj is a quaint town with stunning oriental architecture and an Ottoman feel. It is listed as a UNESCO World Heritage Site, despite being heavily damaged during the 1991–5 war. The town holds the longest operating art colony in southeast Europe, which reopened in 2003 after ten years of inactivity due to the war. Artists from around the world came here to paint the likes of the figs and pomegranates that grow in abundance on the hills of Počitelj.

Dadži-Alija Mosque has been reconstructed, as has the Sisman Ibrahim-pasha's Medresa and the Gavran Kapetanović House. All of

Počitelj settlement in the Neretva Valley

these places are open to visitors. The most impressive architectural object in Počitelj is the Kula, a silo-shaped fort that towers from the top of the hill above the town. This housed watchmen and military who were guarding against possible invasion from the Neretva Delta. All of Počitelj is open, but there aren't many indications to point you in the right direction through the maze of winding stone steps. The café and restaurant at the old *Hamam* (Turkish bath), just below the mosque, serves excellent food and cool drinks.

To get to Počitelj, take bus No 41 from Mostar to Čapljina via Počitelj. Počitelj is about half an hour's drive from Mostar, less than 30km (18^1/$_2$ miles) south on the M-17 road towards the Croatian coast.

Tourist information. Tel: (036) 397 352. Email: hercegovina@hercegovina.ba

Počitelj is worth visiting to see the Kula fort

Serbia

Serbia has been a vital crossroads between East and West for many centuries, and it is still the main thoroughfare for travel between Western Europe and the southern Balkan states of Greece and Turkey. This strategic geopolitical position once placed Yugoslavia as a regional powerhouse and now finds Serbia struggling to secure its territorial sovereignty and move towards European integration.

BELGRADE

Belgrade was once the largest city and capital of the former Yugoslavia. With its disintegration, which started in the early 1990s, Belgrade and Serbia have gone through dramatic transformations. Still very much engulfed in political quagmire, Belgrade struggles to redefine itself politically. Much to the surprise of many travellers, however, Belgrade is a culturally and socially fascinating town. It is rich in both culture and nightlife, and has recently found its way on to many travellers' Eastern European itineraries.

Belgrade is a city of over 2 million people. Situated on the open Pannonian plains where the Sava River flows into the Danube, its position has made the city vulnerable to a wave of invaders since before medieval times. This is best illustrated by the two fortresses of Kalemegdan

that gaze over the two waterways from their hilltop homes. More than any city in this western Balkans guide, Belgrade is a beacon of culture with many great museums, royal palaces, and all that you would expect from a major capital city.

Old town and city centre

Until the end of the 17th century, the old town area was the heart of Belgrade. Situated between the main fortress and Kalemegdan Park, it enjoys splendid views in all directions, and most of the old town's medieval and baroque city walls are well preserved. The squares, parks and numerous monuments attest to the city's long and tumultuous history. After the Turkish departure in 1867, much of the old town was remodelled with a more European urban spacing.

Today, the old town is the most interesting quarter of Belgrade, and

The imposing Kalemegdan Fortress in Belgrade

the easiest to get around. There are cafés on every corner and a wide selection of cultural venues, all within walking distance. If your time in Belgrade is limited, spend it in the old town.

The city centre houses many of Belgrade's museums and theatres. This is the political and administrative centre of Serbia, with its parliament buildings and main squares where the world witnessed the resistance movement that eventually overthrew the regime of Slobodan Milošević. The centre is not as compact as the old town, but it is well connected with trams and bus services.

Kalemegdan complex

The rocky ridge complex that sits high above where the Sava and Danube

King's Gate, Kalemegdan

rivers meet was once the urban centre of old Belgrade. This complex occupies the entire ridge, which has great views of new Belgrade, Zemun and the vast agricultural plains around Belgrade. Kalemegdan's massive complex was the centre of city life during Ottoman and pre-Ottoman times. Aside from the fortress, where World War I began when Austrian forces opened fire after the Sarajevo assassination of Franz Ferdinand, this spatial complex consists of a significant part of *stari grad*, or the old town. The main entrance to the medieval fortress is on the eastern side, near Belgrade's present-day city zoo, through the Zindan and Despot gates. Knez Mihailova and Uzun Mirkova streets lead directly to the Kalemegdan/ Belgrade Fortress. The best way to explore Kalemegdan is to use one of the maps sold at tourist stands around the city.

Kalemegdan Park

This was a no-man's-land during the Turkish occupation of Belgrade. This large field separated the old town from the fortress, enabling Turkish troops to see and stop any opposing forces that might come their way. *Kale* means 'fortress' in Turkish and *meydan* means 'field'. After the Turks' hasty departure, the fields were converted into a park. Today, the rather large park is frequently visited by both students and pensioners. Just outside the fortress walls, Belgrade's newest festival, the Belgrade Beer Fest, is held (*see p19*).

Konak kneginje Ljubice (Palace of Princess Ljubica)

Prince Miloš built this small palace for his family in 1831. Fearing the Turkish authorities, he quickly had a change of heart and moved his residence to another estate in Topčider, to the south of Belgrade. He left the house to his wife, Ljubica, and his children.

The palace is largely oriental and Ottoman in style, with some elements of European design, and included a *hamam* (Turkish bath), as was the custom of the time. After being turned over to the Museum of Belgrade, some redecorating was done to convert many of the rooms to contemporary European style. The basement hall is used for contemporary exhibitions by the museum.

Kneza Sime Markoviça 8. Tel: (011) 638 264. Open: Tue–Fri 10am–5pm, Sat & Sun 9am–4pm. Closed: Mon.

Kosančićev Venac

The winding cobblestone streets that follow the baroque-era city walls are a rare reminder of what the quaint

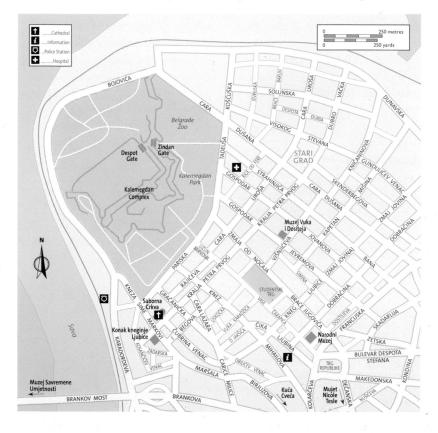

neighbourhoods of Belgrade looked like in the 19th century. This small neighbourhood runs parallel to the Sava River. It is a pleasant and quiet place for a stroll, but has no exceptional cultural value except for the bust of Ivan Kosančić, the knight who allegedly killed Sultan Murad in the epic Battle of Kosovo in 1389. This date, more than any, is a thorn in Serbia's side as it signified the beginning of almost 500 years of Ottoman rule.

Kuća Cveća (The House of Flowers)

Some think that this house should be renamed 'The House of Shame'. This former memorial to the late president of Yugoslavia, Josip Broz Tito, was partially pillaged and confiscated by the Slobodan Milošević regime. The only part of the memorial centre now open to visitors is the white marble grave in the green garden behind the former museum. For history buffs or admirers of the man who managed to hold Yugoslavia together for almost half a century, it's a humbling place to visit.

Muzej Savremene Umjetnosti (Museum of Contemporary Art)

Due to its location near the Sava and Danube rivers and its peculiar diamond shape, this museum is a recognisable landmark. The museum's collections of paintings, sculptures and creative installations deal with artistic creations from the early 20th century

to the present day by Yugoslavia's most acclaimed artists.

Ušče bb. Tel: (011) 311 5 713/5 771/6971. www.msub.org.yu. Open: Mon–Fri 10am–6pm, Sat & Sun 10am–1pm.

Muzej Vuka i Dositeja (Vuk i Dositej Museum)

Vuk Karadžić (1789–1864) and Dositej Obradović (1739–1811) are two of Serbia's most revered intellectuals and philosophers. Karadžić, proclaimed as the inventor of the Serbian Cyrillic language – he standardised the alphabet – dedicated his life to promoting his language skills to the peasantry, while Obradović was among the first Serbian intellectuals to break from the strict teachings of the Church and led Serbia's philosophy of enlightenment movement. The museum

Nikola Tesla

NIKOLA TESLA

Most Westerners believe that it was Thomas Edison who discovered electricity. Well, if you ask anyone in the former Yugoslavia they will certainly tell you otherwise. Nikola Tesla, a Croatian-born Serb, was one of the southern Slavs' greatest scientists. He emigrated to the United States and soon found himself working alongside Thomas Edison. Tesla apparently sent Edison his findings, which he believed to be a life-altering discovery. According to his diary entries, he was convinced he had discovered electricity – and that some of his findings were used by Thomas Edison, who took the credit for inventing what became possibly the greatest innovation of the 19th century.

displays letters, books, portraits and other personal items of these two prominent Serbian intellectuals.
Gospodar Jevremova 21.
Tel: (011) 625 161.

Narodni Muzej (National Museum)

At the onset of the NATO bombing in 1999, most of the pieces in this museum were removed to preserve the country's richest collection of Serbian and European art. After being closed for several years, the museum, which was founded in 1844, was restored and reopened in 2005. The museum is dedicated to painting and sculpture, so it doesn't really present the cultural and natural heritage of Serbia as the name might suggest.
Trg Republike 1a. Tel: (011) 624 322.
Open: Mon–Fri 10am–6pm.
Closed: Sat & Sun. Admission charge.

Muzej Nicole Tesle (Nikola Tesla Museum)

The Serbs tend to get a little irked when history books give credit to Thomas Edison for inventing electricity. There is a unanimous opinion that the great inventor was indeed Nikola Tesla, a Serb from Croatia. After his death, much of Tesla's personal belongings were brought to Serbia and given to his only heir. His heir founded a museum dedicated to the legacy of this brilliant inventor. Alongside Tesla's personal belongings are working models of his scientific discoveries, a library of his works and an archive of documents that he left behind.
Krunska 51. Tel: (011) 433 886.
www.tesla-museum.org. Open:
10am–6pm Tue–Sun. Closed: Mon.

Obilićev Venac

This neighbourhood, along with Topličin and Kosančićev Venac, is situated along the 18th-century fortifications of Belgrade. The once quiet quarter is now a bustling place due to the addition of two shopping centres and more than a dozen cafés. It is a very popular 'strolling' daytime area with a lively nightlife scene.

Saborna Crkva (Orthodox Church)

During the Ottoman occupation of Serbia, Belgrade was divided into Serbian and Turkish quarters. The centre of the Serbian part of the city was at the intersection of Kralja Petra and Kneza Sime Markovića streets.

In 1841, Prince Miloš decided to build a new church in place of the old wooden structure that was beginning to deteriorate. The new building was not entirely constructed in traditional Serbian Orthodox manner, but it had heavy influences from Habsburg design.

On both sides of the main entrance are the graves of two of Serbia's most revered intellectuals: Vuk Karadžić and Dositej Obradović (*see p50*). Like most Serbian Orthodox churches, the most impressive aspects are the humble yet powerful iconostases. They are the works of Dimitrije Avramović, who was among the first of Serbia's romanticist painters.

This church is sacred to the Serbs, for more than one reason. It is open to visitors most days and, as in most Orthodox churches, no shorts or short skirts can be worn inside.
Kralja Petra 5. Tel: (011) 635 699.

Skadarlija

This old gypsy quarter is located just outside the city walls and was once a run-down neighbourhood. Due to its close vicinity to the National Theatre and the low rental rates, many artists rented flats here in the late 1800s. By the early 1900s, it was transformed into the centre of literary and artistic life in Belgrade. Cafés sprung up all over and today there is a café in almost every old dwelling. Two of the classic old school cafés are the Tri Šešira and Dva Jelena founded in 1832. The lower side of Skadarlija Street is owned by a Belgrade brewery. A little further down is the Sebilj fountain, an exact replica of the original fountain in Sarajevo's Baščaršija. It was given to the city of Belgrade as a gift in 1961 at the first conference of Non-Aligned Nations (NAN).

Trg Republike (Republic Square)

Belgrade's central square was built at the main entrance to the city where the Istanbul gate once stood. It was, like many Ottoman structures, destroyed soon after the Ottomans were routed and had retreated from Serbia. The square was named to commemorate the establishment of the Federative Republic of Yugoslavia in 1945. It was also one of the central squares where many of the prolonged Otpor! protests that eventually ousted former president Slobodan Milošević were held.

To the north side of Trg Republike is the National Theatre. Prince Mihailo, a keen lover of the arts, had the theatre built the year that the

Kneza Mihaila Street

Turks departed from Belgrade. The National Theatre hosts many plays and events, mostly in the Serbian language. The box office at the front entrance usually has information regarding performances, concerts and plays. *National Theatre. Francuska 3. Tel: (011) 3281 333, 2620 946 (box office). Fax: (011) 2622 560. www.narodnopozoriste.co.yu*

Ulica Kneza Mihaila (Kneza Mihaila Street)

Kneza Mihaila was hailed as the ruler who managed to diplomatically expel the Turks from Serbian lands. Much of Serbia's history is measured in 'before' and 'after' Ottoman rule. Serbia's European cultural revolution began in this era after the Ottomans pulled out and most of the cities' European characteristics were inspired by the desire to, for the first time in almost 500 years, engage in European trends. Many things are named after Kneza Mihaila in Serbia, including this, one of its most important streets. The broad street is in direct contrast to the narrow, cobblestone streets of Ottoman design, and is now the country's largest pedestrian zone, lined with shops, cafés, restaurants and bars. Kneza Mihaila Street will take you from Trg Republike all the way to Kalemegdan Park.

Ulica Kralja Petra (Kralja Petra Street)

Kralja Petra Street is one of Belgrade's most central and oldest communication lines. It was once the shortest route between the Sava and Danube rivers and, until the creation of Kneza Mihaila Street, it was the city's most vital commercial street. The highlight of Kralja Petra Street is the ornate Orthodox Cathedral.

DAY TRIP FROM BELGRADE
Ada Ciganlija

This river island has become one of the favourite haunts for Belgradians. Ada is a river lake that was formed from a branch of the Sava River. On one side it is bordered by forest and open green meadows, and on the mainland side by marinas and a bohemian cultural centre.

Ada is by far the largest and most popular outdoor recreation area in the region. The lake is a swimming hole and is used for water polo, rowing and even sailing competitions. During the summer, large crowds gather here for watersports events, concerts, or cultural entertainment. In fine bohemian fashion, the marina is lined with houseboats owned by local artists, and there are many restaurants and cafés right on the water. Ada is also an ideal place to bring the family; there are large picnic areas, horse and carriage rides, tourist trains, and canoes and pedal boats for hire. *Ada Ciganlija is 4km (2^1/$_2$ miles) from the city centre of Belgrade, and can be reached by a relatively cheap taxi ride.*

NOVI SAD

Novi Sad is Serbia's second-largest city after Belgrade, and the provincial capital of Vojvodina. The long, flat plains of the Danube and mild continental climate have made this region one of the richest agricultural spots of greater Pannonia. Novi Sad literally means 'New Planting'. The city itself has been coined Serbia's Athens because of its long and rich cultural heritage. Vojvodina finds itself at yet another Balkan crossroads, this time between those of the Catholic and Orthodox Slavs, the Hungarians and a smaller German community.

Dunavska Ulica (Danube Street)

In the old days, Dunavska Ulica was the only street that extended all the way to the river. Back then, the Danube created marshlands that once came much closer to the city centre and Dunavska Ulica was the only access that traders had when bringing their goods via Europe's most navigated waterway. It is no surprise, then, that present-day Dunavska Ulica is the best and most popular shopping area in the city. Some of the shops are still owned and operated by the descendants of the original shop owners. With the street still running from the town centre all the way to the Danube, this is a great place for shopping or for a leisurely stroll along the banks of the river where there are many beaches, cafés and restaurants. At the very beginning of Dunavska Ulica is the house known as At the

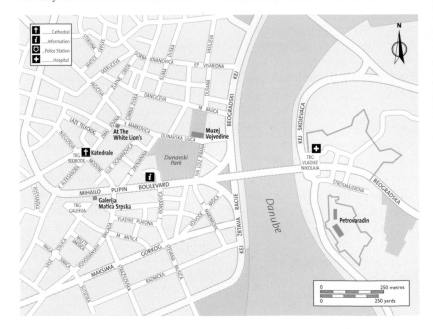

White Lion's (Kod bijelog lava). The house is believed to be one of the oldest in town, dating back to 1720. In 1790, the first printing press house was opened in the house by writer and scientist Emanuillo Jankovic. Keeping with tradition, the house is now the City Library. At No 29 is an open art gallery/museum of sorts. It hosts the Collection of Foreign Art (*Dunavska 29. Tel: (021) 451 239. Open: Tue–Sat 9am–4pm. Closed: Mon & Sun*) that was donated to the city by one if its wealthy intellectuals. The gallery exhibits some surprisingly good art, with paintings by artists like Rembrandt and Rubens.

Dunavski Park (Danube Park)

The old marshlands were transformed into a nicely cultivated park at the end of the 19th century. Located at the end of Dunavska Ulica (Danube Street), this is now one of the most beautiful parks in the city. The pond, home to many swans and ducks, has a tiny island in the centre on which a weeping willow was planted in memory of the Austrian empress Elizabeth. The park marks the ending of the Austro-Hungarian era of influence in Novi Sad, as it was the first park built after the liberation. The park is popular all year round for walks and strolls, and in the summer it is a favourite gathering place for friends and families.

Katedrale (Cathedral)

This neo-Gothic Catholic cathedral replaced the 18th-century one that stood in the same square for over a

Statue in Danube Park, Novi Sad

century. The cathedral was rebuilt at the same time as the City Hall, from 1893–5. Aside from the imposing 76m (249ft) bell and clock tower that is visible from most places in Novi Sad, the cathedral's roof construction is in a unique multi-coloured Zsolnai ceramic style. Czech and Hungarian artists created the beautiful stained-glass mosaics inside the cathedral. The cathedral is open for visitors.

Muzej Vojvodine (Museum of Vojvodina)

Just opposite the Danube Park is a turn-of-the-20th-century former courthouse. In 1966, it was converted to the Museum of Vojvodina. The museum is separated into two buildings. The first building, No 35, is dedicated to archaeology and

Novi Sad clock tower

prehistory, with illustrated exhibits from the Palaeolithic age up to the Ottoman-era occupation. The other entrance, at No 37, deals more with contemporary history, right up to the NATO bombing of 1999. Among the most interesting archaeological collections are items from the Gomoglava dig site, antique frescoes from the Beska necropolis and late-Roman ceremonial helmets.

Dunavska 35–7. Tel: (021) 420 566. Mon–Fri 9am–4pm, Sat & Sun only for prearranged groups.

Petrovaradin

Petrovaradin is by far the most recognisable tourist attraction in Novi Sad. Well known for its EXIT music concert (*see p19*), this beautiful Roman-era fortress defines the lovely character of the frontier town. Originally named Cusum, the Romans used this fortress to safeguard its Danube frontier. From the 11th to the 13th centuries, the Hungarian and Byzantine empires fought numerous battles to control the region. When the Hungarian king Bela IV finally prevailed in 1237, it was called Petrvarad (Peter's Castle), which was later adjusted to its present name in Serbian.

There are many ways to climb the fortress; the shortest and easiest is up the stairs from St George's Monastery. To the right is a climbing tunnel path that eventually leads to a viewpoint of the Danube and the whole of Novi

Sad. The old clock tower dates back to the mid-18th century; you'll notice that the minute-hand shows hours and the hour-hand shows minutes. According to old superstitions, hours were more important than minutes, hence the right of way was given to the hour hand!

Petrovaradin is a multi-functional complex nowadays with hotel and catering facilities. Local artists often display and sell their work here, particularly during the summer season. The EXIT music fest, the largest of its kind in southeast Europe, is held every summer, attracting tens of thousands of music-lovers from all over Europe (*see p19*).

Trg Galerija (Gallery Square)

This tiny and somewhat hidden square just off Mihailo Pupin Boulevard is well deserving of its name. Within a stone's throw of the square there are three of Novi Sad's best galleries: Galerija Matica Srpska and the memorial collections of Rajko Mamuzic and Pavle Beljanski *Galerija Matica Srpske, Trg galerija 1, tel: (021) 421 455. Open: Tue–Thur 9am–3pm, Fri 9am–3pm & 4–8pm, Sat 10am–1pm. Closed: Sun & Mon.*

Trg Slobode (Liberty Square)

This old trading market was once shared by the German community that lived to the west of the square and the

View of Petrovaradin, where the EXIT Festival is held

Serb community residing to the east. It is now the city's central square, dominated by the statue of Svetozar Miletic, who was a former 19th-century mayor of Novi Sad and leader of Vojvodina's Liberal Party. Trg Slobode, like most central squares in the region, is the heart of the city. From here, in all directions, most attractions are walkable, and the hub of the historical town and shopping areas are all nearby. Trg Slobode is also a common meeting place, and there will always be a flurry of people in and around it.

DAY TRIPS FROM NOVI SAD
Fruška Gora National Park

Fruška Gora, meaning 'Frankish Mountain', was made into a national park in 1960 for several reasons. The natural and geographic aspects are rather fascinating. This narrow and isolated natural monument stems from

Velika Remeta monastery

the vast and flat Pannonian plains. It was often the frontier during the Frankish campaigns to conquer the area. The park encompasses an astonishing 25,000sq km (9,653sq miles), with various degrees of protection. Although the park has great ecological significance for the region, it is best known for its monasteries and wine. Most likely due to its geographic positioning, an astonishing 16 monasteries have been built in this area, starting as far back as the 12th century. Coupled with the best vineyards, Fruška Gora offers the best of Vojvodina's cultural and natural heritage.

The most popular monastery destinations are in and around Sremski Karlovci. Krusedol Monastery, which is about 7km ($4^1/_3$ miles) from Sremski Karlovci, was built in 1509 by the Brankovic family. The monastery was originally intended to be a mausoleum for the Brankovic ruling family but it gained even greater importance when in the 18th century it became the seat of the Karlovci Metropolitan. Many of the precious relicts were burned during the 1716 conflict between the Turks and the Austro-Hungarians, and after the Croatian Ustase plundered the place in World War II, most of the remaining icons were moved to Belgrade. This monastery still holds much architectural and sentimental value to the Serbs and is the most visited of the 16 monasteries in the park. If visiting Sremski Karlovic, be sure to try some of the wines; they are the region's best.

Velika Remeta, originally a 13th-century monastery, is located in a beautiful wooded area. It is famous not only for its tranquil settings but for its baroque towers dating from 1765. They are the largest of the Serbian Orthodox monastery bell towers in the park. Grgetec Monastery is also a popular spot because of its iconostasis which was painted by Uros Predic in 1902.

Although its highest peak reaches only 539m (1,768ft), Fruška Gora is an ideal place for hiking, walking and taking long bike rides. Lake Ledenci is also a popular destination in the park's central highlands.

There are dozens of walking areas, and many of the monasteries are linked with good walking paths or along small country roads. The most popular is the Beocin Monastery walk, which goes through Osovlje and Orlovac and finishes in Crveni Cot. It's about a three-hour walk and is relatively easy with an altitude climb of around 400m (1,312ft). From Hotel Venac to Iriski Venasc is a harder walk of about four hours, but the route climbs only 300m (984ft). The trail leads through the New and Old Hopovo monasteries.

There are several tour operators in Novi Sad that offer trips to the national park and the Mountain Association offers hikes to the park every Sunday of the year.

Železničar Association of Mountaineers, Trg galerija 4. Tel: (021) 529 978.

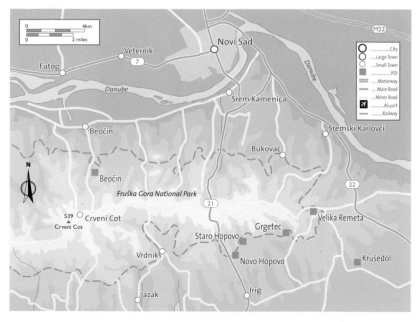

EXIT Festival

Not much in the Balkans has brought about such a wave of positive publicity as the EXIT music festival in Novi Sad. Just as the Sarajevo Film Festival was born in the midst of Europe's longest siege in modern history, the EXIT Festival was a grassroots movement opposing the oppression of the Slobodan Milošević regime in 2000. Novi Sad was known for its opposition to the regime and for being one of the most liberal regions in the former Yugoslavia.

The first EXIT Festival had clear political connotations and was largely organised to send a subtle message to Belgrade. Two students from the University of Novi Sad, Dušan Kovačević and Bojan Bošković, bravely organised the festival through the students' union and several non-governmental organisations (NGOs). What started out as a localised artistic youth rebellion has turned into one of Europe's largest and most cutting-edge music fests. It has, however, stuck to its grassroots origins and tries to bring current social issues to the forefront every year.

EXIT is held in the Petrovaradin Fortress (see p56). The venue itself is enough to excite music fans, let alone the amazing line-up of some of Europe's best bands.

The 2000 festival had a largely local character, but the following year saw nine foreign bands although still no big-name bands. In 2002, EXIT gained considerably more international attention, and the main stage acts were Asian Dub Foundation and Transglobal Underground as well as previous EXIT performers. The nine-day extravaganza had 250,000 guests.

The 2003 festival witnessed a shift in the main stage performers. Organisers targeted popular groups

The EXIT Festival draws in young music-lovers

Crowds gather at the Petrovaradin Fortress

like the Rollins Band, Stereo MC, Chumbawamba, Soul II Soul and many others with more international recognition. This set the stage for even bigger names to roll into town. However, the 2004 EXIT Festival was marred with political scandal when the organisers were targeted and accused of embezzlement of concert revenues. After a large outcry, the founders of EXIT were imprisoned for seven days but released with no charge. That year, however, was one of the best festivals to date. A new Balkan Fusion stage was created to highlight the best regional music, and the main stage brought Massive Attack, Iggy and the Stooges, Cypress Hill and the Wailers to Novi Sad. The biggest names in DJ-ing also made their EXIT debut and included Howie B, X-Press 2 and Timo Maas.

When BBC Radio 1 announced that it would cover EXIT live in 2005, the festival began to wake the music world up. The festival hosted White Stripes, Fatboy Slim and Underworld. Due to the BBC coverage, flocks of young Brits came to Novi Sad in 2006 where the greatest musical festival in the history of the Balkans was held. Billy Idol, the Cult, Morrissey, the Pet Shop Boys and the Cardigans played the main stage. All in all, there were 22 stages with over 600 performers during this grandiose occurrence. The festival has given Novi Sad a new name in music, and given the region's youth something to dance about.

ZLATIBOR

In translation, Zlatibor means 'Golden Pine'. The name was inspired by the rare golden pines (*Pinus silvestris*) that grow in the fir-tree forests here. The golden pine is now an endangered species in the 200sq km (77sq mile) mountain holiday area, but that hasn't stopped Zlatibor from becoming the most popular nature getaway in all of Serbia. This mid-range mountain, averaging about 1,000m (3,281ft) above sea level, is rich in springs and mountain streams. With over 100 caves identified in the area, it is assumed that Zlatibor is one of the most complex karst fields in the country.

The varying landscapes add to the attraction, and the lower altitude makes for ideal climate conditions. There is an even mix of large green meadows and thick forests, and a charming chain of small villages that dot the hillside, with an ever-growing tourism infrastructure that has attracted people from all over Serbia to build their holiday homes there.

The region has a good selection of hotels and B&Bs as well as traditional restaurants and plenty of cafés. The central recreation area has a pool, sports grounds, bike rentals and hiking gear. All of these facilities are within the general vicinity of the many hotels found on Zlatibor. During the summer season, there are daily open-air markets selling both fresh produce and handicrafts from the villagers. You can also find some of the region's best homemade spirits, called *rakija* and generally made from plums. In winter time, there are three ski lifts operating and excellent cross-country skiing trails with rental shops in the centre. Although the mountains are very high, there are still a few months of good skiing conditions, especially for family outings with kids as the slopes are small and not extremely challenging.

The best walking and hiking areas are at Murtenica ridge. This was known during Ottoman rule for the *hajduks* (rebels) who hid from the Turks in this forested area. Cavlovac peak, covered in dense forest, is home to bears, wolves and foxes, and offers great views of the whole area.

For village visits, Gostilje is just 30km (19 miles) from the Zlatibor tourist centre. The village has a lovely

Traditional house, Zlatibor

waterfall and good accommodation. Dobroselica and Jablanica are well-preserved, old-style villages that still have log churches that were popular in the rural areas many centuries ago. Sirogojno is the most popular village, and besides being well known for its terrific wool knitwear, there is also a well-organised ethno village here called Staro Selo where traditional-style Serbian houses have been restored to their original form. There is a great souvenir shop, a restaurant serving food from the village, and occasional open-air theatre for traditional folklore dances, and accommodation in Sirogojno. The area's largest cave, Stopica pecina, is near Rozdanstvo village. It is located along the Pristavica River Canyon and extends over 2km (1 1/4 miles) with dome vaults up to 50m (164ft) high.

Zlatibor's beautiful landscape

Mokra Gora and the steam train

Mokra Gora is a tiny and picturesque mountain village near the border with eastern Bosnia. In pre-war times, Mokra Gora was just another stop along the popular Belgrade–Uzice–Sarajevo railway service that ran from 1925–74. It was a small and rather insignificant village that was practically unknown to most.

However, what was known about the place was the engineering feat of Sargan 8. Stumped on how to resolve the problem of passing over Sargan Mountain near Mokra Gora, engineers decided to construct the tracks in the shape of a figure eight to enable the steam locomotives to climb and descend the 300m (984ft) difference along this rugged stretch of the railway. The *Cira* steam train was adored by Yugoslavs. It was the main mode of transportation for villagers, business people, soldiers, schoolchildren and traders for travelling throughout western Serbia and into eastern Bosnia and Sarajevo. It also hauled livestock, building supplies, fruit and vegetables, mail, ammunition and whatever else needed transport to this isolated mountainous area. This all ended when the old railway from Austro-Hungarian times was put out of use

in favour of a more modern railway system in the mid-1970s. Or so everyone thought.

In 1999, a revitalisation project to renovate the Sargan 8 began. The Mokra Gora–Sargan Vitasi connection is a 15km (9^1/3-mile) long route that travels through 22 tunnels and over 10 bridges. The views and rides are amazing, and locomotive-lovers from around the world have come to visit, or perhaps revisit, this great engineering feat and revived piece of history. The local government didn't stop there though. With the help of international NGOs and the famous Sarajevo-born Serbian film-maker Emir Kusturica, a sustainable tourism development programme started in Mokra Gora.

The old railway has been further expanded, reaching the Bosnian town of Visegrad. Visegrad became famous through the novel by Ivo Andrić, the Nobel Laureate winner, *Bridge on the Drina*. The railway travels via Dobrun Monastery on the Bosnian side and finishes in the centre of historical Visegrad. Now, the old steam train idea is a two–three day tourist adventure for the young and old.

In post-war Serbia, Mokra Gora sparked the interest of many largely

The railway has been restored to its former glory

due to Kusturica's film *Life is a Miracle*. The film was set in this pristine natural area and opened the eyes of many to the value of the traditional architecture and lifestyles of rural Serbia. Kusturica financed the building of a 'replica' village in the vicinity of Mokra Gora in 2002, and built a restaurant and an Orthodox monastery. In the village itself, traditional restoration began with the help of the international community. The roofs were restored with specialised wooden shingles, and the same or similar building materials were used to refurbish crumbling walls.

All of this is now the main tourist attraction in this western border region. The tiny village has almost become a pilgrimage site for some Serbs. The local villagers maintain their traditional lifestyles and are able to make a living by selling handicrafts, providing private accommodation and selling food to the restaurant that serves wonderful traditional dishes and spirits.

VRNJAČKA BANJA

Spas in the western Balkans do not always meet the standards of those in the West, but Vrnjačka Banja (Vrnjačka Spas) is Serbia's best and main spa resort. Settled in the low foothills of Goc Mountain, this spa has six major thermal springs. There are good facilities, with pleasant outdoor environments and a few parks for walking, biking and swimming. For winter travellers, there are ski tracks and a rather small lift that operates on the mountain. Many spas in the former Yugoslavia have excellent thermal and mineral water quality but mediocre services and accommodation. Vrnjačka certainly ranks among the better spas, as does Terme Ilidža just outside of Sarajevo (*see p35*).

Be sure to check out Belimarkovic Castle just above the main pedestrian path. It was constructed for a Serbian general in a similar style to the villas of northern Italy, and is now a cultural centre and gallery. The town organises many cultural events, including the 100 days 100 events festival (*see p19*), and several of the entertainment venues are located in the castle. A film script writers' festival is also held here, hosting Serbia's best film-makers and rising stars (*see p19*).

In comparison to Western costs, the thermal spa treatments and accommodation in Vrnjačka are very affordable. If you have been travelling for a while or trekking in some of the higher mountains, Vrnjačka is an excellent place to stop for a relaxing hot spring treatment.

Vrnjačka is close to the south of Kraljevo and is accessible via the main road.
Serbian Spas and Resorts Association, Poštanski fah 51. Tel: (036) 611 110. Email: banje@ptt.yu

---

MANASIJA MONASTERY

Although not the most important of Orthodox monasteries in Serbia, this certainly ranks among the most impressive. The monastery near Despotovac southeast of Belgrade, marked by 11 towers and old moats, was the bastion of south Slavic Orthodox philosophy starting in the early 15th century. It was home to the famous scholar Constantine the Philosopher, who greatly influenced the literature and language of the southern Slavs. The great walls that protect the monastery were breached as early as 1439 by the overpowering Ottoman army. In the following centuries, the monastery was used more as a fortress than as a sacred place, but since Serbian independence it has once again become a centre for Orthodox monks.

KOPAONIK MOUNTAIN

Kopaonik Mountain is Serbia's most popular ski centre and is one of its highest mountain ranges. The massif, located in the near geographical centre of the Balkan Peninsula, offers the most extensive view in the country from its highest peak, Pancicev Vrh, at 2,017m (6,618ft). From this vantage point, you can see almost half of the territory of Serbia and Montenegro.

Kopaonik belongs to the Central Dinaric Alps, and has over 1,500 plant species. It is blessed with a rich array of forests, and thick beech, fir and spruce cover large parts of the mountains up to the 1,600m (5,250ft) mark. At this point, the range turns into high Alpine pastures which enjoy the most protection. In the valley areas, there is a low zone of willow and poplar trees.

The ski centre has a local feel to it, and it cannot be compared, for example, with the Olympic ski centres of Jahorina and Bjelašnica in Bosnia and Herzegovina. There is a good infrastructure, with large hotel capacities and good access all year round. The ski lifts are a little outdated, but they have several good runs.

Kopaonik is great for hiking and trekking. There are many well-marked trails, and the favourable climate provides a long season of outdoor activities on the mountain. There are occasional sightings of eagles, wild cat, deer and wild boar on the mountain

STUDENICA MONASTERY

Studenica Monastery near Kraljevo is the most important and sacred of all Serbian monasteries. It was here that Saint Sava, who established the independent Serbian Orthodox Church, wrote what would become the cornerstone of monastic rule for Serbian Orthodox monks. The monastery was founded by Saint Sava's father, Stefan Nemanja. The Nemanja dynasty was the protector of the monastery from its founding in 1183 until the Ottomans destroyed it in the 15th century. The monastery complex has three churches enclosed by a beautiful stone wall. It is open for guests all year round.

range. The ski centre is the best place for summer accommodation, and there are full recreational facilities for guests.

GUČA GORA BRASS BAND FEST

Inspired by the great tradition of gypsy brass band music, this festival in southwest Serbia draws in a large number of gypsies, hippies, Serbian nationalists and just plain music lovers in what can only be described as an outdoor orgy of great brass band music. Taking place every year at the end of August in the town of Guča Gora, the festival has begun to gather international acclaim as a love for gypsy music in Europe continues to grow. If you are travelling in the region around this time it is worth going, as it is a truly unique music festival.

Jelovarnik waterfall, Kopaonik Mountain

Montenegro

Montenegro is a tiny but fascinating and diverse country. It has recently begun to realise its full tourism potential and has become one of the newest and most exciting destinations in Europe.

The coastal region is blessed with an array of dramatic landscapes. The northern and central areas, around the towns of Kotor and Budva, have a towering backdrop of impressive mountains, while the areas to the south, near Ulcinj and Ada Bojana, have wide, sandy beaches.

The central region around the capital, Podgorica, comprises the vast open valleys between the coastal and rugged northern areas. The climate, terrain and vegetation are influenced by both Mediterranean and Alpine factors. The cultural capital, Cetinje, has warm, dry summers, yet the mountain streams and thick forests of Lovćen Mountain mean the winters are wet.

The area from Podgorica to Niksic is the most densely populated region in Montenegro, and it is also the industrial heart of the country. Its closeness to the Adriatic, however, gives it a more Mediterranean feel than an Alpine one. Lake Skadar, south of Podgorica, is by the far the most beautiful, and is the 'tourist' highlight of the central region with an amazing collection of flora and fauna.

Travelling through the Moraca Canyon just north of Podgorica, the landscape turns to the 'rough and tough' that Montenegro is famous for. Deep canyon gorges, jolting Alpine peaks and thick conifer forests dominate the northern landscape. It is a different world from the sunny and relaxed atmosphere of the Montenegrin coast to the south.

Montenegro

The natural beauty of Lake Skadar

Montenegro

KOTOR AND BOKA KOTORSKA (BAY OF KOTOR)

There are undertones of local rivalry about which is the most beautiful coastal area in Montenegro. Kotor and the Budva Riviera, although very close to each other, always seem to be vying for the title. Both have a very different feel to one another. Kotor and its bay, the southernmost fjord in Europe, is an ancient trading centre with a rich maritime folk culture. The old city was founded in the 8th century and is perhaps the best-preserved medieval town on Montenegro's Adriatic coast. Its beautiful architecture and numerous cultural heritage monuments have warranted UNESCO to list it as a World Natural and Cultural Heritage Site.

Very often the Balkans are seen as the crossroads between Christianity and Islam. What many may forget is that this vital geopolitical peninsula was also the crossroads of the Byzantine and Roman influences. Kotor best represents this unique intersection, highlighted by the Catholic and Orthodox monasteries on the two islands in the Boka Kotorska (Bay of Kotor). In the old town itself there are many medieval churches, namely the 13th-century St Luke's and Holy Mary churches.

The rich combination of Illyrian, Roman, Gothic, Byzantine and baroque cultures has shaped this charming town. Kotor preserves a medieval Mediterranean feel more than any other town in the country. You can almost sense the era when pirates ruled the sea and large city walls were erected to protect Kotor from this vulnerable and well-travelled stretch of the Adriatic.

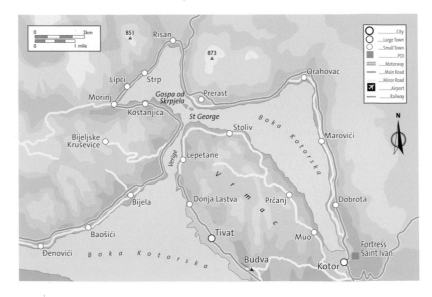

Like any ancient maritime settlement, Kotor is steeped in folklore and superstitions. The most significant celebration in Boka Kotorska has taken place since the 9th century. This tradition honours St Tripun, who died a martyr during the Roman Empire in the 3rd century. The cult-like commemoration of St Tripun is very strong in Kotor, where it is believed that on 13 January 809 a ship carrying the relics of this saint was brought into the bay. Shortly afterwards, a church was built in the saint's honour by a local nobleman. On top of this medieval foundation is the symbol of this city, St Tripun's Cathedral. Every January a celebration is held at the church to commemorate the protector of Kotor and the symbol of Montenegro's oldest and largest maritime community.

Fortress St Ivan

Worth a trip purely for its photographic value, this fortress offers impressive views of Kotor and the bay. It is located just above the walls of the old town of Kotor and is reached via the winding road from the east entrance to the city. Known better to the locals as St Djovani (St Giovanni), the fortress sits at 280m (919ft) above the sea, with a magnificent panorama of the entire area. It's a bit of a steep climb, but there are several resting spots along the way.

Fortress St Ivan

Maritime Museum

The Maritime Museum gives an interesting glimpse into Kotor's past. It is a source of great local pride and many of the exhibitions have more of a sentimental value than historical significance. The ethnographic collection is quite interesting as are some of the old geographic charts and nautical maps.

Bokeljska Mornarica Square. Open: Mon–Fri 9am–5pm, Sat 9am–noon.

Old town

Although not as well known as the famous neighbouring city of Dubrovnik in Croatia, Kotor too has fabulous and grandiose city walls that stretch 5km (3 miles), encircling the entire old city. At certain points the walls are 20m (66ft) high and 10m (33ft) thick. Construction of the city walls began as early as the 9th century and the fortifications lasted another ten centuries. There are three main gates to the city and all lead to the most significant and revered building in the city – St Tripun's Cathedral.

Trg od Oruzja (Arms Square) must have been a trading point for weapons to defend the city. Today, it is the city's largest and most popular square. Not only a gathering place, the square is a central point from which to visit many of Kotor's best cafés and shops. You'll find both locally owned and operated shops and world brand-name shops here. From here, it's easy to find some of Kotor's most significant architectural objects, like the 8th-century watchtower, the 17th-century Duke's Palace and the 19th-century Napolean's Theatre.

Prerast

Even though Montenegro, and particularly Kotor, has seen drastic growth as a tourist destination, the tiny town of Prerast is known as the most beautiful and peaceful settlement in the bay. The well-preserved narrow alleys with Renaissance and baroque residences testify to the town's wealth during medieval times. Most of that wealth came from the sea, as almost the entire population of Prerast consisted of seamen and traders. Today, it has roughly 350 inhabitants, making it an ideal spot to get away for a quiet day.

Kotor's old town

You can wander the well-kept streets and admire the 16 palace residences. There are no beaches to mention in Prerast, but it is a great place for a day trip or as a launching point to the island of Gospa od Skrpjela.

BOAT TRIPS TO THE ISLANDS OF GOSPA OD ŠKRPJELA AND ST GEORGE

Not far from Prerast and an easy boat ride from Kotor, these two islands make great day trips. Gospa od Škrpjela is a church on an artificial island built of rock and superstition. Legend has it that fishermen from Prerast miraculously discovered an icon of the Virgin Mary, which inspired them to build a church here, and they did so in 1630. Many centuries later, the island still inspires the 'festival' Fasinada. This upholds a tradition of throwing rocks into the sea to widen the surface of the island and preserve the ancient altar that exhibits the icon in the church. Every 22 July, superstitious locals in Prerast can be found throwing rocks into the sea.

St George, also known as Dead Captain's Island, has not escaped ancient folklore either. There are several versions of the story, but it is said that a French captain, firing a shot towards Prerast, accidentally killed his

The islands of St George (left) and Gospa Od Škrpjela (right)

lover. He then either died or shot himself on the island. This legend inspired the Swiss painter Belkin's masterpiece *Island of the Dead*.

Although there are strange legends surrounding the islands, they are situated in the heart of the Bay of Kotor, which is certainly one of the most beautiful places on the Montenegro coast. This fjord has stunning mountains on three sides and is truly one of a kind. Regular boats from the port or tourist boat 'taxis' on the coast run regular trips to the islands.

BUDVANSKA RIVIJERA (BUDVA RIVIERA)

Many consider Budva and its 21km (13 miles) of coastline to be the highlight of Montenegro's seaside

Mogren beach, Budva Riviera

tourist destinations. The area has 17 beaches, many islands and several small bays. The old town of Budva is labelled by the locals as a 'treasure chest' of cultural heritage. In fact, the old town is not only charming but hosts a magnificent variation of old Mediterranean architecture. Stari Grad, or the old town, is located on a small peninsula that darts out into the crystal-clear Adriatic.

Budva is believed to be the oldest settlement on the Montenegrin coast. The natural and cultural history of this place is a fascinating one. Budva is first mentioned in the 5th century BC in Greek records. However, the occupation of the Roman Empire for so many centuries left a largely Venetian influence on the town's architecture. Geographers tend to favour the theory that Budva was once an island that was later joined to the mainland by a sand isthmus. The shape of the old city reinforces this idea, with defensive walls that indicate that the town was indeed an island.

Although Budva is located only a few dozen kilometres from Cetinje, the city was only briefly part of the Montenegrin state during the 19th century and early parts of the 20th century, falling mainly under Austro-Hungarian control. It wasn't until the formation of the Kingdom of Yugoslavia in 1929 that all the various Slavic enclaves that were under occupation were united.

Today's Budva is a rather small settlement of 10,000 inhabitants. However, it receives 250,000 tourists each year – making tourism by far the most important industry for the region's inhabitants. Aside from its many beaches and inspirational old town, the Budva Riviera is famous for its nightlife. Cafés, clubs and beach parties are a constant from May until late October, and the town's many festivals turn the place into a big party for most of the summer. The Mediterranean Song Festival is by far the most popular, with a week's long manifestation of local and regional Mediterranean tunes.

Many of the cultural sites are open to guests. The ethnographic museum (*tel: (086) 52 137*) just touches the antiquity of the town's long history.

Most exhibitions display archaeological finds with old vases, jewellery and eating utensils, but there are also some great historical maps and ethnology timelines of Hellenistic, Illyrian, Roman, Byzantine and Venetian influences on the region. There are two churches in Budva that were originally built in the 7th and 8th centuries – Sveti Ivan and Sveta Marija are among the oldest basilicas in Montenegro.

Bar

This port city is not famous for its sandy beaches or deep fjords, and it is often left off the itineraries of many travellers to Montenegro. Bar connects Montenegro to Italy, Albania, Greece and Croatia by ferry boat. If you are travelling by ferry around the Adriatic,

Old town, Budva

Bar is a great hub to spend a day in before or after your journey. The city centre has a great nightlife scene, and at King Nikola's Castle along the coast, which is also a museum, there are often concerts and events.

The old town of Bar, mainly abandoned and under restoration, was a medieval gem. Because of pirates, the city was built almost 5km (3 miles) from the sea at the base of Rumija Mountain. Although largely uninhabited today, it's an amazing place to visit and it's hard to understand why the revitalisation of this precious medieval town didn't start long ago.

Because of its large port, Bar doesn't have many beaches in the town itself. Sutomore is the local riviera, only a few kilometres from Bar. It is a typical Adriatic riviera, with long pedestrian walkways, plenty of cafés, and a good selection of guesthouses. Just a few more kilometres up the road is a great camping site at Ratac. There are camping facilities for both camper vans and tents and there are nice beaches in the near vicinity. Ratac is isolated and quiet enough that parts of the beach have become nudist.

Petrovac

This tiny settlement on the halfway point between Budva and Bar is a very pleasant place for a quiet holiday. Originally a fishing town, Petrovac depends largely on its tourism industry. Located on a sandy bay, it is surrounded with pine forests and olive groves. This alone is its greatest attraction for those looking for a peaceful and pleasant beach holiday. The main beaches are about 500m (547yds) from the main *riva* (road), and are usually quite crowded with guests. However, as in most places along Montenegro's coast, there are always small, hidden coves for a quiet swim for those who care to explore. There are a decent number of guesthouses and more than enough cafés and eateries along the *riva*.

Sveti Nikola Island

Known by the locals as 'Hawaii', Sveti Nikola is one of Montenegro's best island hops for getting away from the Riviera crowds. You can reach the beaches and numerous capes by taxi boats which are available in Budva harbour. A great place for a quiet day trip or a mini adventure, you can explore the whole island and its rich flora and fauna. There are deer, wild hare and many species of birds, as well as rare plant life and the classic Mediterranean herbs of sage, rosemary and lavender. Much of the island is covered with thick spruce and pine forests, making walking and exploration more bearable during the summer heat.

In your wanderings, you may come across a part of the island that has been privatised. It may sound like an odd concept, but a part of the island was bought and is now being developed as a private beach resort.

Sveti Stefan (St Stephen's)

Sveti Stefan epitomises the 'jet set' resorts that are popping up along the Adriatic coast. This picture-perfect resort town was built in the 15th century by tradesmen and fishermen. In the 1960s, its ideal location, wonderfully preserved medieval architecture and rich plant life gave two famous Montenegrin painters, Petar Lubarda and Milo Milunovic, the idea of a high-rolling resort town. By 1972, Sveti Stefan was crowned the best exclusive summer resort in the world with a 'Golden Apple' award. Since then, the town has been transformed from a summer residence of the local nobles to a world-class, upmarket getaway for the likes of Sophia Loren, Princess Margaret, Ingemar Stenmark and Sylvester Stallone, to name just a few.

Most of the accommodation on the island-like settlement is highly exclusive. Some of the villas start from 1,500 euros per night. Don't be discouraged by accommodation rates, though; the small and narrow Mediterranean streets are like a scene from a movie, and the beaches, squares and cafés are worth a day's visit if you're on the Budva Riviera. Despite the hype and stardom of Sveti Stefan, it still has a somewhat laid-back atmosphere, albeit a glamorous one. For a taste of the high life, a stroll through town or enjoying Montenegro's version of high-street shopping and dining are memorable experiences. Sveti Stefan can be reached by foot as it is connected to the mainland by a narrow sandy strip.

Montenegro

The resort town of Sveti Stefan

Skadarsko Jezero (Lake Skadar)

Lake Skadar is named after the city of Shkodra (Skadar) in Albania. This national park extends across the border to Albania, where a third of the lake's territory is located. Out of the 391sq km (151sq mile) surface area of the lake, about 220sq km (85sq miles) fall within Montenegro's border. The park itself covers 40,000ha (98,840 acres), including several marsh areas and small fishing villages along its shores. The underground karst aquifer systems of the Dinaric Mountain chain create the world's largest and most unique limestone fields of their kind, stretching from Slovenia all the way

to Albania. From historical records it is thought that the Lake Skadar area was once only a river region, with many sources and river systems that fed the Adriatic. At some point in time, one or many of the aquifer systems must have closed, creating one of Europe's largest natural lakes.

The lake is lined with idyllic villages and surrounded by low mountains. From almost anywhere on the lake, there are outstanding views. Lake Skadar strikes most people as a place of harmony; there is a quiet balance between people and nature here. About halfway down the lake on its western shore is Murica beach, a favourite swimming hole for the locals with a pebble beach alongside a sleepy village. The tiny islets here are great for fishing as are the northwestern ends of the lake near Rijeka Crnojević. This once booming trading and fishing town is once again an isolated settlement that time seems to have forgotten. Boat trips are offered from many of the towns on the lake, and often include Beska Island monastery to the east of the lake. Sveti Dorde is a 15th-century Orthodox monastery; there are frequent sightings of owls here and

Lake Skadar is good for birdwatching

Peaceful and natural Lake Skadar

rock doves are always circling and diving overhead.

With over 270 types of bird species, Lake Skadar is not only one of Europe's pristine bird sanctuaries but is becoming a bird-watchers' haven. The Dalmatian pelicans make their homes in the reed-filled marshlands. Curly pelicans (*Pelicanus crispus*) have nesting grounds near the border with Albania, and these are the only ones recorded in Europe. Grey herons have founded a nesting colony on Omerova Gorica Island among the laurel trees. Black Ibis and pygmy cormorant are also commonly seen. In the winter months, thousands of migratory birds flock to the lake region on their long journey from Europe to Africa.

The lake is home to over 50 fish species. Carp and trout are the most common fish here, but even some saltwater species make their way upstream from the Bojana River. Eel and sea bass have both been caught in the lake.

The lake is accessible from all sides, and the most popular boat launching areas are around Virpazar. This small fishing village has accommodation, restaurants and boat tours during the high season (June–September).

CETINJE

Cetinje has always had a significant meaning for Montenegrins, as the country's original capital. Lately, however, its historical and sentimental value cannot be underestimated. With Montenegro's newly found independence, there is now talk of moving the capital from Podgorica back to its original location – the Cetinjsko fields at the foot of Lovćen Mountain. Cetinje was founded by Ivan Crnojević after fleeing from the Turkish invasion between 1482 and 1485. Since that time, Cetinje has been the sacred centre of Montenegro.

During King Nikola's rule from 1860 to 1918, much of the present-day city centre was built. In this era, the king constructed embassies, residences, and medical and educational institutions that gave Cetinje a very European flavour. Most of the churches and monasteries were built before then, with the oldest Orthodox monastery dating back to 1485. The cultural heritage of Montenegro and its ruling aristocracy can be witnessed in the many museums that line the wide streets in the compact city centre. In fact, the city now has more museums and cultural heritage sites than any other place in Montenegro.

Like most western Balkan cities, Cetinje has a thriving café culture, but one that is quite different from the coastal areas. Surrounded by Lovćen Mountain, the views offer both forested and dry, arid landscapes.

Cetinje is a sort of lonely oasis in the Cetinjsko fields, creating a sense of the isolation that Montenegro experienced during the countless Ottoman attempts to root out the kings and finally conquer the nation.

Cetinje is a perfect place to be based for a few days, enjoying both the city and Lovćen National Park (12km/7^{1}/$_{2}$ miles away with regular and accessible transport to the park and its attractions).

Cetinje Monastery

If you head towards the King's Castle in Cetinje and turn right, you'll soon come to what is considered the most important religious centre in the cultural capital. Cetinje Monastery was originally founded in the same year as the city was established as the new fortress by Ivan Crnojevic in 1485. The reconstructed monastery was completed in 1701 and is a wonderful example of Orthodox mysticism. The icons and design are impressively beautiful and, unlike many Catholic sacred places, Orthodox design has maintained its original flavour dating back to the Byzantine Empire. The church and monastery are open to visitors and there is a souvenir shop where you can buy many authentic and handmade gifts.
Tel: (086) 31 021.

Ivanova korita (Ivan's River Bed)

Ivan's River Bed is located on the River Trestenik. Due to its rich water sources it is thought that the founder of Cetinje, Ivan Crnojević, built this large stone reservoir and funnelled water to Cetinje via hollowed-out beech logs. This area is dense in forests and has large green Alpine meadows that are a favourite picnic and walking spot for both locals and tourists. There is a restaurant and facilities that are open year round.

12km (7¹/₂ miles) from Cetinje, on the road towards Lovćen National Park.

Njegoš' Billiard Pool Hall

It may seem strange that the home of Montenegro's most heralded statesman and philosopher is now a pool hall, but that is certainly the case.

Once the residence of Petar II Petrovic Njegoš and called New House until billiards arrived in Cetinje, it has since been known locally as 'Njegoš' Billiard Pool Hall'. However, it resembles more of a medieval castle than a pool hall. The house has 25 rooms, the most famous being Njegoš' pool hall – where Njegoš apparently spent a lot of his time. The first pool table came to Cetinje from Vienna in 1839 and has been used by Montenegro's nobility since then. Today, the house is not an active pool hall but a museum of the entire residence that is highlighted by Njegoš' love of billiards.

Novice Cerovića 66. Tel: (086) 231 303, 231 682. www.heritage.cg.yu

Montenegro

Cetinje Monastery was founded in 1485

River Crnojević

Njegoš' mausoleum walk

Even though this mausoleum is situated in a very beautiful natural environment, it is important to understand how much Petar II Petrovic Njegoš is revered by the Montenegrins. Njegoš was a 19th-century poet, statesman and philosopher who nurtured and defended Montenegro's national identity.

He is the most important figure in Montenegrin history and part of the Petrovic dynasty that ruled Montenegro for centuries. Visiting his mausoleum is a pilgrimage of sorts for many local people. It is apparently the highest mausoleum in the world, located at Jezerski vrh at 1,660m (5,446ft), and provides a cool break from the heat of the lower-lying areas.

The trail to Njegoš' mausoleum is lined by beech and oak forests and is only 13km (8 miles) from Cetinje.

At the mausoleum there is a parking area with a restaurant, toilet facilities and a souvenir shop. After paying a small entrance fee, a guide will offer you more information than you could possibly imagine about Njegoš and the construction of his resting place. Be prepared to walk up 461 stairs as well and to do a bit of climbing. The views of Lovćen Mountain are well worth it, and the restaurant Vidikovac (Scenic View) is a nice resting spot for a coffee, drink or lunch.

Njegošev mauzolej, Jezerski vrh.
Tel: (01) 4648 007.
Email: info@llc-eco-adventureagency.hr

Njeguši

Njeguši is the birthplace of Petar II Petrovic Njegoš and most of the Petrovic dynasty. The house of Njegoš' birth has been converted to a museum, but the taste of real country life may appeal more than the museum. This small settlement with about 50 houses is famous in the region for its smoked ham, speciality cheese and high-quality honey production. At 900m (2,953ft) above sea level, between Cetinje and the coast, the conditions are also perfect for growing grapes and producing the local firewater, *loza*. There are several restaurants and guesthouses in Njeguši and neighbouring Bukovica.

River Crnojević

This once vital and bustling trading centre and winter royal residence has returned to being a tiny and sleepy settlement. The River Crnojević is a stunning natural oasis just 16km (10 miles) off the main road from Cetinje to Podgorica. There is no public transport to this place, but for nature-lovers it is worth hiring a car or guided tour to the area. The river and its surroundings are pristine, and up until the Balkan wars this was a trading post inhabited by Muslims, Orthodox Christians and Catholics alike. Today, it is a small fishing village and a great place to visit for nature photography, walking and canoeing.

Njegoš' mausoleum is located at Jezerski vrh

ULCINJ

This southernmost Montenegrin city is situated in an open plain near the Albanian border. It is one of the least-known attractions on Montenegro's Adriatic coast, but it is quickly gaining in popularity due its charming medieval city, the 12km (7¹/₂ miles) of sandy beaches, and the country's most diverse bird populations at the migratory habitat of Lake Sasko.

It is widely believed that the Illyrian tribes that once inhabited the entire Balkan Peninsula settled the area of Ulcinj as far back as the Bronze Age. The city itself is thought to have been founded by Greek colonists in the 5th century BC. The Romans left their mark as well, as they did on the entire Adriatic. With the arrival of the Slavs, within a relatively short span of time most of the Montenegrin Adriatic saw the indigenous Illyrian tribes absorbed

by the larger and dominating Slav ones. Ulcinj, however, largely maintained its indigenous population. It is supposed in many academic circles that the Albanians are the last remaining descendants of the original Illyrian tribes. If this holds true, Ulcinj could very well be a 2,500-year settlement of the same indigenous tribes.

Old Ulcinj, just a few kilometres from the heavily fortified medieval old town, was known for a very long time along the Adriatic as a pirate town. Trading ships often went far out of their way to avoid raids by the lawless pirates, and many riches are claimed to have been lost at the hands of Ulcinj's bandits. Today, Old Ulcinj has much more of an oriental feel to it, and there is a heavy Ottoman influence in the city. The small cobblestone streets lined with Turkish-style handicrafts workshops and cafés offer a rare oriental ambience on Montenegro's coastline. It's a great place to buy handmade crafts, listen to ethnic and folk music or hear the 'live' call to prayer from the city mosque. Most visitors spend at least a day in these oriental quarters.

Regardless of its history, Ulcinj's population is now mainly Albanian. It is a popular tourism destination for many Albanians from Kosovo, and attracts the large diaspora populations from Europe and North America. More and more Europeans are finding it to be a good, and less expensive, Adriatic holiday spot.

Fishing at Ada Bojana beach

Ulcinj's old town, like most along Montenegro's coast, encompasses many layers of cultural influences that go back thousands of years. The original architects were certainly the Greeks and Romans. The Turkish fountain and 12th-century Orthodox churches, however, are evidence of significant Byzantine and Ottoman influences in the city.

Dvori Balšića (the Balšića Tower), located behind the old museum, is now used partly as a gallery. It is the best example of the ingenuity of medieval architecture in Montenegro. The Ethnological Museum is just a few metres away, with some interesting exhibits but nothing spectacular in its own right. In the same area is the former slave square, with the vaults still there that used to hold the slaves before they were sold. One of the most luxurious structures in the old town is the 14th-century Palata Venecija – the finest example of Venetian architecture built during the high point of the Venetian Empire's influence in the Adriatic region. Although the old town has plenty of interesting things to see, it is not organised in a way that will allow you to get the most from your visit.

Dvori Balšića, Ethnological Museum, Palata Venecija. Stari grad.
Tel: (085) 421 457.
www.touristinmontenegro.com. Email:
dvoribalsica@touristinmontenegro.com

Ada Bojana (Bojana Island)

In the mid-19th century, the trading ship *Merito* was grounded in the shallow waters where the Bojana

The old town of Ulcinj

Ada Bojana is an important centre for watersports

River meets the Adriatic Sea. After many decades, the sand and sediment from the river began to form an artificial island around the ship. This sediment build-up eventually expanded to engulf two small islands in the inlet, creating what is today known as Ada Bojana – one of Montenegro's most famous beaches.

This unique sandy beach now covers almost a 3km (1³/₄-mile) strip and has become a haven for watersports enthusiasts and nudist beach-goers. This southern stretch of Montenegro's coast, close to the Albanian border, enjoys a nature reserve status due to its dense and diverse vegetation. The main attraction, however, is the tropical-style atmosphere that the rare sandy beaches have created.

The beaches, lined with reed huts, have become the hotspot for windsurfers, boaters and waterskiers. There is a windsurfing school run by certified guides that provides professional training for those seeking a thrilling watersports adventure. Ada Bojana is also one of the rare places on the Adriatic where you can find horse-riding.

The river bed shores are lined with traditional fishing cabins where flocks of local fishermen make their living by providing local restaurants with the fresh catches of the day. The traditional seafood restaurants here boast that they are among the best in Montenegro and offer an interesting array of both salt- and freshwater fish dishes. Waiters often give the best advice on which daily fish special to indulge in.

Ada Bojana is located on the main road south of Ulcinj.

Lake Sasko

This is a bird-watcher's paradise. Located in the general vicinity of Ada Bojana, this 364ha (899-acre) lake is a migratory bird oasis and home to storks, herons, geese and cormorants. Although not well organised, there are opportunities for wooden canoe-like rides on the lake. Going out on to the lake offers a much better chance to see some of the region's rarer birds and nesting areas.

Valdanos Cove

This is an olive grove oasis tucked in a wind-protected cove just a few kilometres from Ulcinj. The groves produce immense amounts of olives and some trees are believed to be over 300 years old. The trees provide much welcomed shade along the rocky beach at the base of the cove. The water here is calm and crystal clear, making it an ideal place for snorkelling and exploring. Legend has it that many shipwrecks were washed into the cove, and it is now a favourite place for divers and snorkelling enthusiasts. There is a restaurant and bar on the beach as well as toilet facilities.

PODGORICA

Podgorica was reduced to rubble after German bombing in World War II.

The Millennium Bridge at Podgorica

Montenegro

Although Podgorica was only a small settlement, emerging from the war with 4,000 inhabitants, most traces of the town's history were erased. Just after the war, reconstruction began, and within the new Yugoslavia, Podgorica – formerly Titograd – would become the new capital of the Republic of Montenegro. Tito embarked on a massive plan to build a city and to connect it with other parts of Yugoslavia, namely Belgrade. A railway was built through the rugged and difficult terrain of the north to reach the coastal areas, and the roads programme of the 1960s and 1970s connected Titograd, for the first time, with asphalt roads to other Yugoslav cities.

Podgorica has dramatically grown since then and is by far Montenegro's largest city, with close to 200,000 inhabitants. The tourism value of Podgorica is limited, although it does

Podgorica's 10th-century Orthodox church, St George's

offer an interesting glimpse of a provincial capital that is now the capital city of one of Europe's newest states. The Montenegrins are very proud of that, with this sentiment quite strong in Podgorica.

Like most places in the region, there is a strong café culture. The 'old town' of Podgorica is a newer old town, granted, but quite lively. There are dozens of cafés and many modern bars and boutiques; the best are along the Hercegovacka pedestrian street in the centre.

The old Turkish town, Stara Varos, bears witness to the Ottoman influence. There is a mosque and a typical *kasaba* or *mahala* (neighbourhood), with narrow cobblestone streets lined with workshops. St George's church is perched on Gorica Hill, to which Podgorica owes its name. This 10th-century Orthodox church offers a good view of the city. King Nikola's castle has been converted to a museum and the grounds are a park. Although the museum lacks any great content, the castle and grounds are nice to visit.

If you like city life and prefer to do day trips, Podgorica is centrally located as a base. Lake Skadar is quite close, as are Cetinje to the west and Ostrog Monastery to the north. A short day trip can be made to the ancient settlement of Medun, just 10km (6¼ miles) from the centre of Podgorica. The ruins of Duklja form the oldest Roman settlement of its

Podgorica's City Hall

kind in the region, dating back over 2,000 years.

Podgorica also serves as a great transport centre if you are travelling through the region. The city is well connected and well situated for the lake district and coastal areas as well as the northern territories. There are regular buses to Serbia and Bosnia and Herzegovina. The international airport in Tivat is only a 15-minute drive from the centre and a short ride from the coast. The train station connects Podgorica to the north all the way to Belgrade. The ride is slow but the scenery is incomparable. The rail and bridge system just north of Podgorica in the Moraca Canyon is a major feat of engineering and, for those afraid of heights, a nerve-racking experience.

Ostrog Monastery and St Vasilije

Few people expect to witness such a marvellous spectacle when they arrive at Ostrog near Nikšić. Intricately carved into the rising limestone rock face at Ostroska Greda, the Ostrog Monastery is considered by many to be the most beautiful and inspiring Orthodox sacral place in the former Yugoslavia. You can hardly argue with those views.

The monastery has become the largest religious pilgrimage site in the country, with many Orthodox Christians coming from Serbia, Bosnia and Herzegovina, Macedonia and the wider Orthodox world. Even many local Muslims pay homage to St Vasilije, the founder of the 17th-century monastery, and go there for healing. St Vasilije died in 1761 and was later named a saint by the Serbian Orthodox Church. It is believed that by praying near his shrine and burial spot, miracles are known to happen.

St Vasilije was born in Popovo Selo, a small village in southern Herzegovina very near the Montenegrin border, on 12 December 1610. He became a monk and served at Tvrdos Monastery in Popovo Polje, near Trebinje. A modest and well-liked monk, Vasilije turned down his first offer to become Bishop of Zahumlje and Skenderija. He eventually accepted. His life was dedicated to helping the poor and healing the sick, and he became well known throughout the entire region. When he died, Vasilije was buried in the monastery that he founded in Ostrog.

The present-day structure was built in 1923 after a fire destroyed a large part of the original complex. Its architecture is astounding, a perfect blend of the splendours of human and natural creations. The original two caves that were used as a place of worship were spared from the fire, and they are the spiritual core of the monastery. The frescoes, many of them originals from the 17th century, were painted along the contours of the cave – creating a fascinating harmony that dominates this place.

Throughout the year there are many organised events, mainly revolving around the Orthodox Church calendar. The monastery has become so popular that it has constructed dormitories where worshippers or the simply curious can spend the night. It is open to visitors all year round, for all religions and denominations, and there is no entry fee. The souvenir shop has an interesting variety of spiritual and

Ostrog Monastery is located on a rocky mountain range

religious gifts as well as locally produced spirits. The shop supports the work and lives of the monks living there.

The quickest and easiest way to Ostrog from the coast is via Podgorica and Danilovgrad to Nikšić. The monastery is well marked once approaching Nikšić. If you're up for a small adventure from Herceg Novi, there are many back roads that climb through the hinterlands near the border with Herzegovina. The views are fantastic and the roads wind through a maze of isolated highland villages. The roads are all paved and well marked on relevant maps. Ostrog is also a good stop-over before heading to Zabljak or carrying on to Bosnia and Herzegovina via Scepan Polje.

Ostrog Monastery, Poštanski fah 16, Nikšić. Tel: (081) 811 133.
Free admission.

Getting away from it all

The western Balkan region is a nature lover's paradise. Most of the area is situated in the heart of the Central Dinaric Alps – one of Europe's least explored mountain ranges. Although you may have to look a bit harder, it's well worth the effort when it comes to rural tourism and enjoying the traditional lifestyles and cuisine of the highlands. There are more and more B&Bs being established in mountain villages, as well as small guesthouses that offer accommodation food and light outdoor activities.

BOSNIA
Neretva River rafting

The southern slopes of Bjelašnica Mountain near the town of Konjic end at the Neretva River. This crystal-clear mountain river has become one of the most popular white-water rafting destinations in southeast Europe. The long and fun journey stretches over 26km (16 miles) and takes around 4–6 hours to raft. The Neretva is a class II river making it safe for children as well; the minimum age is ten years old. This deep river canyon has stunning scenery and to make the trip even more amazing, the river water is so clean it's potable for most of the trip. Europe Rafting offers professional guided tours with all the necessary safety equipment (*Tel: (061) 817 209.*

The Neretva River

Sunset at Hutovo Blato Bird Reserve

Getting away from it all

Email: info@raftingeurope.com.
www.raftingeurope.com).

HERZEGOVINA
Boat ride: Hutovo Blato Bird Reserve

Hutovo Blato Bird Reserve is the largest of its kind in southeast Europe. This part of Herzegovina has an abundance of natural wonders. Hutovo Blato is home to over 240 types of migratory birds and dozens that make their permanent home in these sub-Mediterranean wetlands surrounding Deransko Lake, only a few kilometres from the sea. It is estimated that up to 10,000 birds at one time flock to the lake in the winter months. This marshland is created by the underground aquifer system of the Krupa River. It is fed from the limestone massif of Ostrvo that divides the Deransko and Svitavsko lakes.

The park rangers will take you on a fascinating *barco* (boat) ride through the reedy marshlands, narrow canals and crystal-clear lakes. The wildlife has a unique oasis among the harsh arid karst of western Herzegovina. Teeming with freshwater fish (trout, carp, sunfish, grey mullet and eel), wild duck, geese, coots, hawks, herons, pheasants and wild boar, it accommodates bird-watchers, nature-lovers and families with children.

The International Council for Bird Protection placed Hutovo Blato on the list of important bird habitats. January and February are the best months for bird-lovers, as these are the main months for bird migration to Africa. *This nature reserve is located only 5km (3 miles) from the city of Čapljina, just off the main M17 road. Open: all year round. Free admission. The boat ride lasts for up to 2 hours.*

Continued on p100.

Sutjeska National Park and Tara River rafting

Sutjeska is one of Bosnia and Herzegovina's oldest parks. It is famous for the Partisan victory over the Germans in World War II, and there are large stone monuments commemorating the event. The park itself is 17,500ha (43,243 acres) of magnificent wilderness. It hosts Perućica, one of the last two remaining primeval forests in Europe. Beech trees tower over 55m (180ft) high, and endemic black pines stem from the rocky faces that protect the ancient forest. The Skakavac Waterfall can be seen from the lookout point – this 61m (200ft) waterfall is dwarfed by the massive blanket of green trees that covers the valley.

Sutjeska River has carved a stunning valley through the middle of the park and divides Zelengora (Green Peaks) Mountain from Maglić and Volujak mountains. Bosnia and Herzegovina's highest peak, Maglić at 2,386m (7,828ft), is located in the park, directly on the border with Montenegro, and presents a challenging climb for experienced hikers. The park has a hotel in Tjentište (the flat valley along the River Sutjeska) and a café and restaurant. Hotel Mladost (see p159) is socialist in style and not particularly attractive, but the nature within the park border competes with that found anywhere in Europe. Zelengora Mountain is great for hiking and walking, and there are several newly renovated mountain huts on the mountain. Bear and wolf sightings are common. The

Wild horses in Sutjeska National Park

park, although maintaining its pristine nature, is not well organised in terms of marked paths, good maps or visitor information, but you can hire a guide for a day.

For eons, the powerful flow of the Tara River has hollowed out a soft limestone surface, creating the sculpted forms of gorges and chasms that are seen today. Age-old earth erosion has created the 82km (51-mile) long canyon, the second-largest canyon in the world after Colorado. At its deepest, the canyon walls are 1,300m (4,265ft) high. In a few places, the Tara River gives the impression that its furious flow is beginning to calm, but it always gathers momentum and continues its dramatic course to the Drina River.

Along the river banks, the vegetation is very dense: black pine, eastern hornbeam, black ash, elm, linden and, in higher areas, cork oaks, hornbeams, maples and beech trees. Fir and spruce forests grow in the areas above the 1,000m (3,280ft) mark. The black pine forests of endemic species are of special interest. *Crni pod*, or the black floor at the bottom of the canyon, is home to unusually tall trees. Some stretch as high as 50m (164ft) and are over 400 years old.

Aside from nature-lovers and fishermen, the river attracts a large number of adrenalin junkies. Rated at class II/III, it offers some of the most intense and challenging rafting in Europe. A ride on one of the 'real' rafts – logs tied together and guided by a massive wooden rudder – is quite an experience. There are, of course, rafting outfits that provide sturdy and safe rubber rafts with all the necessary gear. Most groups operate out of Foča (there are also several rafting agencies in Montenegro) and offer breakfast, lunch and overnight camping in their rafting packages.

PK Encijan (rafting tours), Foča.
Tel: (058) 211 150.
Email: encijan@zona.ba.
www.pkencijan.com

RIVERS IN DANGER

One thing that can be said of the western Balkans, and in particular Bosnia and Herzegovina and Montenegro, is that they have an amazing number of crystal-clear mountain rivers. Both countries boast of having some of Europe's most abundant and richest sources of clean water. These two tiny countries are now faced with the dilemma of becoming ecologically colonised – with both Bosnia and Herzegovina and Montenegro having an energy surplus, the EU sees these future members as a vital energy supply source. But inept and corrupt governments in these young nations have plans to build hydroelectric dams on the Tara and Neretva potable waterways. This will cause what most environmentalists are calling the greatest threat to Europe's most biologically diverse region.

Walk: Lukomir medieval village

The Lukomir village walk is one of the most impressive walks in Bosnia and Herzegovina. It offers a perfect combination of the cultural and natural heritage of this country and symbolises the inseparableness of people and nature in this part of the world. At 1,469m (4,820ft), the medieval village of Lukomir, with its unique stone homes with cherry-wood roof tiles, is the highest and most isolated permanent settlement in the country.

To get there, you start the walk in the beautiful and serene village of Umoljani, one hour from Sarajevo, and the entrance to the Rakitnica Canyon.

The walk takes around 4 hours (7km/4 miles). For more information, contact Green Visions (see p159).

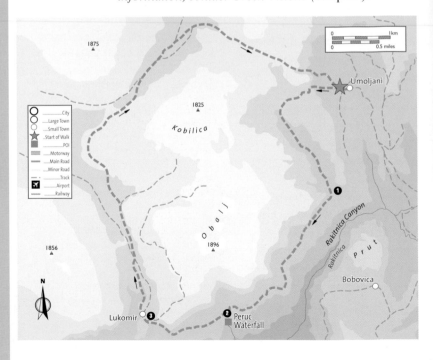

1 Rakitnica Canyon

After half an hour of easy ascension near Studeni Fields, the first breathtaking views of the canyon open up.

From here, the trail leads along the western ridge of the canyon, taking you through thick conifer forests and high Alpine meadows.

2 Peruc

After 90 minutes of trekking, the 50m (164ft) waterfall of Peruc appears from the rocky ridge. This is an ideal spot for lunch or to take a break.

Now the climb up towards Lukomir village begins. You'll pass several ancient water mills and certainly come across a few highland shepherds with their flocks.

3 Lukomir

The views far into the heart of the central Dinaric Alps are remarkable, and the high peaks of neighbouring Visocica and Prenj mountains tower above as you near the medieval village where time has stopped.

Once you reach Lukomir, it is truly like entering a portal to the ancient past. The traditional highland lifestyles here have been untouched for centuries. Enjoy a coffee and meet with the locals, and then you'll be picked up after this stunning 4-hour walk.

Sheep pens in Lukomir village

Walk: Lukomir medieval village

Olympic ski centres

One of the beauties of skiing or hiking in Sarajevo is the proximity of the mountains to the city centre. The 14th Winter Olympic Games in 1984 were one of the largest and most successful of their time. Although some of the infrastructure was destroyed during the war of 1992–5, much of that has been reconstructed, and Sarajevo's Olympic mountains are the most attractive and inexpensive ski centres in southeast Europe. There are no high-tech modern lifts or upmarket Alpine villas, but no one can dispute the quality of the slopes, snow and the fun to be had skiing on these mountains.

Jahorina Mountain lies to the east of Sarajevo and is located in the Republika Srpksa entity, while Bjelašnica and Igman are situated to the south of the city not far from the international airport. In terms of summer activities, the mountains are a nature-lover's paradise. There is a great selection of walking, hiking, biking and highland village trips. Jahorina and Igman are also nice areas for picnics or walking, with a limited number of marked trails.

Skiing in the Olympic mountains

Jahorina ski centre
Jahorina is the mountain range to the southeast of Sarajevo. Its ideal geographical position more or less guarantees four months of good snow for skiing. Its highest peak reaches 1,910m (6,267ft), and the ski lifts climb to 1,894m (6,214ft), with fabulous views towards Sarajevo. The slopes of Jahorina are covered in tall pines up to the tree line at 1,500m (4,922ft). It is the country's most popular ski destination, so book ahead if you are thinking of taking a ski holiday here.

The resorts and infrastructure escaped the ravages of war, and several

The ski resort at Bjelašnica

new hotels have been erected in the past few years. There are 12 lifts all over the mountain that offer Olympic-style professional trails and novice trails for children and beginners. The high season on Jahorina is mid-December to late January. An alternative for last-minute travellers is to book a hotel in Sarajevo and drive to Jahorina, as it is only about 45 minutes from town. On the mountain you will find the full range of facilities, including an indoor swimming pool, medical centre, information centres, ski rentals, restaurants and cafés, skiing instruction in English and internet access.

Bjelašnica and Igman ski centres

These two names are linked to the 1984 Winter Olympic Games.

Considerable reconstruction of Bjelašnica has now been undertaken, with the first phase completed in 2006 with the construction of some ski apartments, restaurants and hotels. Igman is still heavily damaged and will take more time to recover. There are, however, great novice ski slopes and ski areas for children, and Bjelašnica and Igman are within the framework of a new national park that is in the final planning stages.

Currently, there are three lifts operating on these mountains. Bjelašnica has a better infrastructure and the most challenging slopes, while Igman is a little easier and has a children's lift with soft hills to practise on.

Trebinje

Trebinje ranks alongside Mostar in terms of beauty. The southernmost city in Bosnia and Herzegovina escaped the ravages of war and has maintained its original look. It is at an important crossroads, with Mostar to the north, Dubrovnik 28km (17 miles) to the west and Herceg Novi in Montenegro a short distance to the south. Despite its close vicinity to Dubrovnik in Croatia, the most dominant influences on Trebinje have been the Serbian and Muslim cultures. Today, the city has a mainly Serb population.

There is not a single town or city in western or southern Herzegovina that was not erected alongside a freshwater river. Trebinje's old town lines the banks of the Trebišnjica River, which flows through the heart of the city. This quarter is a perfectly preserved old Herzegovina town and a great place to walk or to enjoy a drink or lunch.

The Arslanagić Bridge

Just outside of the centre towards the north, this is a magnificent example of Ottoman stone bridge building. Many of these types of structure have lasted centuries without needing repair.

New Orthodox Church, Trebinje

Klobuk

Klobuk is the large fortress in Trebinje. It is thought to date back to the 9th century and it is believed that the Slovenian princes of Krajina, Pavlimir and Tešimir were buried here. From the 12th century, it was in the possession of the Nemanjic region of Montenegro, and in 1377 Klobuk became part of the expanded Bosnian state.

New Orthodox Church

On the hill protruding from the centre of the city is the New Orthodox Church. The road from the hospital leads to the new complex which is open to the public and has a nice, but rather expensive, souvenir shop. The views of Trebinje from here are the best in town.

Trvdoš Orthodox Monastery

The monastery dates from at least the 15th century. It was built on top of another *hram* (sacred place) that is believed to have been from the 5th century. The old architecture and sharp, bright colours of the icons inside are stunning. Set in the floor is a 5th-century tomb that has been covered by treated glass, and what is believed to be a 5th-century fresco was found near the tomb.

The monastery is open to visitors but the wearing of shorts, tank-tops or sandals is not permitted.

Trebizat and Kravica waterfalls

The long green belt that meanders through the dry lands of western Herzegovina is created by the Trebizat River. This large karst area is covered with underground aquifer systems that occasionally surface and feed into the crystal waters of the gorgeous and potable river. The river starts its initial resurfacing near the town of Grude, not far from the Croatian border. As it flows towards the Neretva River, it is fed by a unique system of natural springs that breathe life into this otherwise arid landscape. When it flows southeast past the medieval town of Ljubuški, the Trebizat meets a long wall of limestone rock faces that creates one of the most powerful waterfalls in the country. It stretches over 100m (328ft) across and tumbles down 25m (82ft) into a large pool that has become a favourite swimming hole for locals. There is a large picnic area with a café and restaurant here, and some great spots to pitch a tent. If camping, be careful with campfires and always follow a leave-no-trace policy.

Not far from the picnic area is the launch for the canoe safari that travels along the remaining sections of the Trebizat. An extremely pleasant four-to five-hour canoe ride is manageable, even for children, and a home-cooked meal is served at the halfway point. The canoe ride is refreshing and calming, with only minimum exertion needed to paddle along the tranquil waters of the easy-flowing Trebizat. The trip ends near the mouth of the Trebizat where it flows into the Neretva and eventually the Adriatic Sea.

Canoe M, Struge bb, Čapljina. Tel: (036) 810 585. Email: marinko.previsic@tel.net.ba

Velež Mountain

Not even known to many locals, this far-reaching natural oasis is just half an hour's drive from Mostar. The Podveležje Plateau rests between the towering peaks of Velež Mountain and the city of Mostar. For centuries, it has been home to highland shepherds and a traditional way of life. The landscape is harsh, arid karst dotted with small forests of beech and oak trees. Situated 700m (2,297ft) above sea level, this is a pleasant escape from the hot summer nights of Mostar, and an ideal place for walking, mountain

Velež Mountain

biking, medicinal herb picking and challenging treks to Velež's highest peak at 1,980m (6,496ft).

In the main village of Smajkici, you can witness many of the old methods of traditional life like sheep-shearing, cheese production and honey-making. There are kilometres of asphalted roads across the plateau with almost no traffic, and they make great bike trails. There are also dozens of walking trails made by the shepherds walking with their livestock.

Podveležje has even more sunny days than Mostar does, and the eco-motel Sunce, meaning 'sun', is in Smajkici (*Tel: (036) 560 082. www.motel-sunce-podvelez.com*). The motel is a family-run business with a strong eco slant to its work. The owner can arrange walks and hikes, and local guides can take you to Velež's peaks. The restaurant serves traditional, organic Herzegovina meals in one of the most peaceful settings in the country. The family get all of their food from local farmers, and the house specialities of grilled lamb, *pita* baked under the *sać* (filo-dough pastry dish made with cheese, spinach or potato in a Dutch oven) and homemade soup have received raving reviews.

Local buses (No 16) run from the main bus station in Mostar to Smajkici in the mountains six times per day.

Vjetrenica Cave

This cave is in Zavala in the municipality of Ravno in Bosnia and

Herzegovina. The cave is one of the most interesting phenomena of the Dinaric karst, the largest of its kind in the world. Vjetrenica is unique in its diverse structure, natural phenomena and cultural history.

For more than a century, Vjetrenica has been a tourist attraction, and in 1964 electricity was brought to some 1,050m (3,445ft) of the cave. After a period of ill-repair, much of the infrastructure has been repaired and the cave is now open to visitors. Further research has recently begun and it is expected that Vjetrenica will be placed on the UNESCO natural heritage list.

The cave is 12km (7^1/2 miles) from the Adriatic highway in Croatia and 25km (15^1/2 miles) from Dubrovnik.

SERBIA
Tara National Park

Many parts of the Drina River region, on both the Serbia and Bosnia and Herzegovina side, are relatively unknown, even to many local inhabitants. In recent times, there has been a concerted effort by both local governments and the international

Tara National Park

community to bring light to this undiscovered corner of the Balkans. The Drina River, which originates at the border of Montenegro and Bosnia and Herzegovina, forms a large part of the natural border between western Serbia and eastern Bosnia. The canyon lands that the Drina has carved through time, coupled with several artificial lakes created by hydroelectric dams, have established great fishing grounds and even better havens for nature boat cruises. On the Serbian side of the border, the wealth of the region's natural heritage is largely concentrated in Tara National Park.

Tara Mountain, according to old Slavic legend, got its name from the friendly pagan god Tarr who chose to spend his life there due to its godly natural wonders. Tara National Park is probably the most unspoiled region in the country, with little development and high levels of protection. The park covers an area of just under 20,000ha (49,420 acres) and centres on the Tara

The Drina River is formed by the confluence of the Tara and the Piva rivers

Mountain. The highest peak, Kozji Ridge, reaches only 1,591m (5,220ft) – relatively low compared to most Central Dinaric mountains. The park has a rich array of flora and fauna, and about one-third of Serbia's flora and fauna can be found here. The wildlife in the more isolated parts of the park is remarkable, including the European brown bear, wolves, the protected golden eagle and even the lynx, but it is rarely seen due to hunting in the wider region. Early morning and just before sunset are the best times for viewing wildlife. The park has the advantage of many scenic viewpoints that, with a good pair of binoculars, greatly improve the chances of an animal sighting.

Many people visit the park to observe the endangered species like the golden eagle and *Picea omorika* pines from the dozens of stunning vistas in the Tara Canyon area. The mélange of limestone karst faces and rich pine forests creates ideal landscapes for the park's 80-odd bird species.

The park has two centres, both with adequate accommodation and information services. Mitrovac has a children's recreational centre and a few restaurants; it's a friendly place to bring children and to enjoy safe outdoor activities. Kaluderske Bare has the park's main hotel complex and is the best place to stay. There are three hotels in total in the park, each of them from the socialist era.

Apart from the interesting nature in the park, the region has an old world rural feel to it and the local villagers are very friendly and hospitable. During the summer months, there are local festivities, including sheep-shearing competitions and rodeos, which are quite unique experiences. The local restaurants, although not used to catering to tourists, serve simple but tasty traditional meals. *Located in the municipality of Bajna Basta, the Tara National Park is easily accessible from Belgrade and Uzice in Serbia and from Visegrad in Bosnia from the west. Tel: (031) 851 445. Free admission.*

MONTENEGRO
Biogradska Gora National Park

When the northern parts of Montenegro were finally liberated from Ottoman rule in 1878, the people from Moraca and Rovca gave part of Biogradska Gora to King Nikola Petrovic as a gift and named it Branik Kralja Nikole. This forest then became protected and, in 1952 after the partisan victory, an area of 5,400ha (13,343 acres) became Biogradska Gora National Park.

Biogradska Gora is the smallest of Montenegro's four national parks, but it has a little primeval forest with many trees dated at well over 500 years old. This forest gives life to 26 different plant habitats with 220 types of species. The fauna diversity is just as impressive, with over 150 bird species and 10 kinds of mammals making their home in the park and surrounding area. The forest itself is a dense mix of 86 tree species, dominated by beech, spruce and pine trees. There are well-marked paths through the forest and to the glacier lake which is found at 1,820m (5,971ft).

Although Montenegro has declared itself an 'ecological state', it continues to battle with the dilemma of hunting in national parks. In certain areas of Biogradska National Park hunting is permitted, so make sure you have clear instructions at the park entrance about where you are going. Hiking and mountaineering are the most popular activities here, but the tradition of

The tremendous Tara River Canyon

hunting is difficult to eliminate, even in the most precious and valuable ecosystems in the country.

The park is just off the main road between Kolasin and Mojkovac, and road signs are visible from the main road. Free admission.

Durmitor National Park

The Central Dinaric Alps are quite possibly the most unexplored mountain chain in Europe. Unexplored, that is, by Western travellers. Durmitor Mountain, a national park since 1980, is the mother of all mountains in Montenegro. Durmitor National Park is the natural extension of its sister park in neighbouring Bosnia, Sutjeska National Park, and together these are certainly the largest tracks of pristine wilderness in southeast Europe. Both parks are included on UNESCO's world natural heritage list.

The park is bordered by deep river canyons and contains Europe's deepest river gorge, the Tara River Canyon. This Alpine highland park has 30 peaks over 2,000m (6,562ft). The highest here and in Montenegro is Bobotov Kuk at 2,522m (8,275ft).

The main attraction and the easiest accessible point in the park is Žabljak. Žabljak is the country's highest permanent settlement at 1,465m (4,807ft), and there is great skiing here, usually for a good four months of the year. Cross-country skiing and snowshoeing are also available with a few of Durmitor's tour operators. The ski centre is a regional attraction; it has limited accommodation and difficult access and has yet to put itself on the European ski destination map.

Durmitor has, however, put itself on the hiking, trekking and rafting map of many outdoor enthusiasts. There are several groups organising hiking tours and highland village visits within the national park. The best of these is the local NGO, Most (Bridge), which belongs to a larger network of community activists that not only is trying to protect the area from exploitation, namely the construction of hydroelectric dams and deforestation, but is also attempting to provide alternative means of economic development for the highlanders. This group of young enthusiasts know the mountain extremely well and provide good guiding services from their headquarters on Žabljak. Montenegro Adventures, based in the capital, Podgorica, also organises hiking and trekking trips that often involve a combination of hiking and visits to highland settlements.

The great variation of landscapes and the rich flora and fauna in this region are unparalleled in Europe. Bosnia and Herzegovina and Montenegro are home to well over 3,000 types of flora, with dozens of them endemic to this region alone. Durmitor also has a diverse variety of wild game – bears, wild boar, wolves,

Durmitor National Park's beauty is breathtaking

roe deer, foxes and dozens of bird and fowl species can all be found in the park. Springtime in the park is a wild flower lover's paradise; the high Alpine plains are covered in a barrage of wild flower colours, and medicinal herbs, such as wild thyme, mint and chamomile, grow wild over the entire range.

NGO Most, Vučedolska bb, Žabljak. Tel: (089) 360 010. www.ngo-most.org. Montenegro Adventures, Moskovska (Maxim) 63–64, Podgorica. Tel: (069) 315 601. www.montenegro-adventures.com

Durmitor National Park can be reached from many access points. From the coast, it is best to travel either via Podgorica to Mojkovac and then make

Visit Durmitor National Park

the climb to Žabljak. Alternatively, there are good access roads from the Niksic area close to the border with Bosnia and Herzegovina. From Serbia, the best route is via Pljevlja and the Tara Canyon. The train from Belgrade to Bar also stops in Mojkovac, where you then have to find public transport to Durmitor. Free.

Lovćen National Park

Like many national parks in the former Yugoslavia, Lovćen National Park was granted protected status partly because of its natural heritage and partly because of its cultural and historical significance. Lovćen is a sacred mountain for most Montenegrins and is directly tied to their identity as a people. Located just above the historical and cultural capital of Montenegro, Mount Lovćen was cherished by the Montenegrin philosopher and statesmen Petar II Petrovic Njegoš, and his mausoleum is located in the park at the base of some of Lovćen's highest peaks.

The geographical qualities of Lovćen National Park are rather impressive. The mountain rises from the coastal area and reaches its peak at 1,749m (5,738ft). The mix of warm Mediterranean and cool Alpine climates has created a wonderful and diverse ecosystem. The mountain, similar to those throughout the Dinaric chain, hosts 2,000 types of plant species. This diversity makes for high-quality produce, meat and dairy products, and the villages around Lovćen make some of the best home-grown foods and spirits in the country.

The central activity in Lovćen is first and foremost the pilgrimage to Njegoš' mausoleum (*see p82*). The infrastructure is good and the trails are well marked. Ivan's River Bed is also a popular spot for picnics, and where walkers can spend the day (*see p80*). The two most popular outdoor activities here are walking or trekking and Nordic skiing. Some trails are marked while others are not, so always look out for trail markings. The trails meander in and out of conifer forests and open, rocky terrain typical of Mediterranean climates.

Mount Lovćen is a sacred mountain for most Montenegrins

Tara River

Many people in the western Balkans have a tendency to proclaim things as the biggest and the best, such as the tallest mountains or the biggest waterfalls, but quite often these claims have no foundation. However, in the case of the Tara River, they're absolutely right. The Tara Canyon is Europe's deepest, reaching an awesome 1,300m (4,265ft) at its greatest depth. The Tara River is also Europe's largest freshwater supply, with most of its 144km (89 miles) being potable. This may sound like a staggering figure, but Montenegro and Bosnia possess more clean and potable river water than the whole continent of Africa. Consequently, the Tara River is a UNESCO World Heritage Site and an integral part of Durmitor National Park.

Along the Tara it is quite possible to see chamois hopping along the high cliff walls, or even an occasional brown bear, particularly in the isolated areas along the Montenegro–Bosnia border. The river is endowed with many types of fish, the most abundant being the freshwater trout that may be served for lunch during your trip. The superb colour of the water is attributed to its limestone bed, which not only provides a constant supply of fresh water from underground aquifer systems, but also feeds cleansing minerals that keep the water crystal clear and potable.

There have been recent plans to dam the Drina River in Bosnia, which would flood the most beautiful part of the Tara Canyon and forever destroy this natural wonder. Those plans, at least for now, have fallen through after protests from both sides of the border.

Rafting on the Tara has become a national sport for most Montenegrins,

Tara River Canyon

Rafting on the Tara River

and many have tried at least a one-day adventure from Brstnovica to Scepan Polje. This 18km (11-mile) route is the classic course, manageable by all, taking about three hours and hitting many of the hotspots of the canyon. For those who choose the two–three-day adventure, it's one you won't soon forget. Starting at Splavista, your 100km (62-mile) journey will start at the beautiful waterfalls at Ljutica. You will enjoy amazing turquoise waters and a great abundance of vegetation on the entire trip. Some of the highlights include coasting under a 165m (541ft) bridge, which is the crossroads for Mojkovac, Zabljak and Pljevlja. At times, the river will be a tranquil mirror easing you down its gentle waters, but when the canyon narrows, expect some thrilling rapids. In the summer season, when the water levels are at their lowest, the Tara is a fun class II–IV rafting river. In the springtime, with melting snows from the high mountains surrounding the canyon, there are many class V rapids and wetsuits are required.

There are several qualified and certified outfitters with great skippers. They provide lunch and all accommodation for the longer trips, and lunch and transport for the one-day rafting. From the Montenegro side, you have to pay a large admission fee for the national park as well as the normal rafting fees.
Montenegro Adventures, see p108.
PK Encijan, see p95.

When to go

There are three distinct climate zones within the western Balkan region. The Central Dinaric Alps region in Bosnia, northern Montenegro and western Serbia has continental, alpine climates with a full four seasons and all their characteristics. The central and northern parts of Serbia are in the central European climate zone with four distinct seasons, but with less extreme cold and snowfall compared to the Alpine regions of the Dinaric. Montenegro's coast and Herzegovina enjoy warm and mild Mediterranean weather, and spring starts earlier and winter comes later in these regions.

BOSNIA AND HERZEGOVINA

Having the advantage of sharing two distinct climate zones, Bosnia and Herzegovina has several good seasons for tourism. Herzegovina is within the Mediterranean zone and experiences a majority of sunny days. From early spring to late autumn, the weather is quite favourable. The high season (June–September) is less crowded than the Montenegrin coast, but does experience a significant increase in guests, although not an overwhelming one.

Bosnia's summers are continental alpine – they are hot with temperatures consistently over 30°C (85°F). In the mountainous areas, the evenings are cool and provide a pleasant escape from the day's heat. In late spring and early autumn in the Alpine zone of Bosnia, you will usually experience very nice weather. Winter in Bosnia is rather cold, with temperatures hovering around 0°C (32°F) for many months. The ski centres of Jahorina and Bjelašnica usually start the season in late December and have good skiing into mid-March, on average, but sometimes later.

Snowshoeing on Mount Bjelašnica

SERBIA

Spring in Serbia is the country's most beautiful season. The vast green meadows are covered in wild flowers and the outdoor cafés are swarming with sun-seeking Serbs. The days are warm and usually sunny, with cool evenings. Summertime is similar to many Central European countries; it is rather hot and July and August can be muggy and humid with temperatures in the mid 30s°C (mid 80s°F). Beware mosquitoes in the Danube and Sava regions; they can be quite bothersome. Spring through to early autumn in the more mountainous areas is sunny and comfortable with cool evenings. Without any major ski centres, the winter season in Serbia is much less exciting than in the Dinaric Alps.

WEATHER CONVERSION CHART

25.4mm = 1 inch
°F = 1.8 × °C + 32

MONTENEGRO

Depending on your holiday style, there are many good times of the year to visit Montenegro. The high season is in July and August, and the coastal areas are very crowded at this time, with prices tending to be 10–25 per cent higher. May and June on the coast are extremely pleasant and warm enough for swimming; this time of year is much less crowded than the high season and the prices are lower. September and October are also less crowded and perhaps more comfortable than the high temperatures of July and August.

The northern territories have shorter summers and rather long winters. For hiking and rafting trips, May through to October are good months, and there are rarely large crowds to beat. For skiing or winter sports, December to early March is fairly consistent with good snow levels. Road conditions in the north are often extreme and can be dangerous.

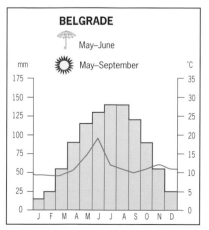

BELGRADE
May–June
May–September

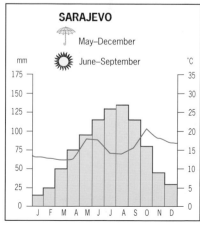

SARAJEVO
May–December
June–September

Getting around

The entire region is connected by a network of two-lane roads and impressive feats of railroad engineering. Due to the mountainous geography, there are few motorways to speak of. Driving can be a beautiful experience, although somewhat daunting and challenging with all the curves, passes and occasional patches of bad road. The bus system in all three countries is very efficient and mostly reliable, but the railway is a less effective way of travelling in the region. Maps can be found at tourist information offices and at most travel agencies and petrol stations. Use caution when travelling at night, as many roads are not very well lit. You should check winter weather forecasts before venturing into mountainous areas.

By rail

Bosnia and Herzegovina

There are now three routes that originate in Sarajevo: the Sarajevo–Zenica–Banja Luka–Zagreb route takes about ten hours from start to finish; the northern route to Budapest via Tuzla; and the southern route towards the Adriatic coast, which takes in Konjic–Jablanica–Mostar–Čapljina–Ploče (Ploče is in Croatia). Getting around by train is slow but enjoyable, and it offers some terrific scenery. Rail is also a comfortable alternative if you are nervous travelling by bus on the bendy roads. Bus and train prices are about the same.

Serbia

Internal rail services are generally poor in Serbia. Services are often overbooked, unreliable, unsafe and slow – especially in winter.
Destinations accessible by rail include Belgrade, Niš, Novi Sad, Priština and Subotica. For further information, contact Serbian Railways (*www.yurail.co.yu*).

Montenegro

Bar, Podgorica, Kolašin, Mojkovac and Bijelo Polje are on the main railway line running to Serbia. Timetables are available from Railways of Montenegro (*www.zeljeznica.cg.yu*).

By car

In all three countries, drivers are required to have either a valid driver's licence from an EU country or an International Driving Licence. No customs documents are required, but green cards and vehicle registration or ownership documents and a locally valid insurance policy are necessary. It is always good to pack a road map before taking a trip, and regional maps are available in newspaper kiosks and most petrol stations. Renting a car is an easy option in all three countries, and most agencies allow you to travel to neighbouring countries (*see p143*).

For repairs and flat tyres, there are plenty of garages. An auto repair shop is called an *auto mehaničar* and a garage that can fix a flat is called a *vulkanizer*. These are usually cheap and will do the job straight away. Spare parts for British-made cars will be difficult to come by. German cars are the most popular and spare parts can be easily found. If you are travelling with your own vehicle, it is always wise

to carry extra fuel, air and oil filters. They are often the cause of car troubles and are easily fixed if you have the parts.

Bosnia and Herzegovina
Travelling by car is by far the most convenient means of transportation to see the country, and you can travel at your own pace. The roads are decent, but don't expect anything resembling a motorway. The rather winding roads often travel through river valleys and over mountains. There are no toll roads in Bosnia and Herzegovina. Road signs in some areas are frequent and accurate, but all of a sudden they can disappear for extended periods of time. Travelling through the Republika Srpska entity can also be a challenging experience as most of the road signs are in Cyrillic.

Getting around

A steam train on the Sargan mountain railway in western Serbia

Serbia

Serbia is the only country of the three to have a proper motorway. The main motorway from Zagreb to Belgrade extends all the way to the border with Macedonia and is the main corridor to Greece and Turkey. There are tolls on the motorway and the roads are usually in good condition. Lighting is often poor, both on the motorway and off. The road systems in the north are generally in better shape than those to the southwest and in the central parts. Some road signs will only be in Cyrillic, but most are marked in Latin script as well.

Montenegro

There are over 5,000km (3,125 miles) of roads in Montenegro. The two major roads are the Adriatic motorway from Igalo to Ulcinj, and the motorway linking the north and the south from Petrovac to Bijelo Polje via Podgorica and Kolašin. Premium and unleaded petrol and diesel are available. Driving at night is not advisable, owing to the poor condition of the roads. Winter conditions, particularly in the north, are very bad. Snow chains are a must, but it is recommended that you limit your travel in the north.

By bus

All three countries have excellent and far-reaching bus services that cover not only their respective countries but the entire region as well. Don't expect information services in English at the bus stations, but a little sign language and patience seem to do the trick. Major bus stations will have daily schedules posted on the wall. Some buses are comfortable and clean, but there are the occasional private bus companies that use rundown buses with broken seats, windows that don't open, no air conditioning and a driver that smokes the entire journey.

Bosnia and Herzegovina

The public and private bus system in Bosnia and Herzegovina is the best available transportation next to having your own car. Literally every town and most villages are connected one way or another by reliable bus routes. Every city and town will have a bus station, and the daily departure and arrival times should be posted on the wall of the station.

A busy road in Serbia

Centrotrans is the main intercity bus line, but there are many bus companies operating throughout the country. It is important to note that inter-entity buses between the Federation and Republika Srpska are less frequent, especially from smaller towns. Sarajevo, Mostar, Tuzla, Zenica, Travnik and Bihać are the main transit centres within the Federation. In the Republika Srpska, the main stations are Banja Luka, Doboj, Bjeljina and East Sarajevo.

Serbia
There are good bus services in the main towns throughout Serbia. Multi-journey tickets are available and sold in advance at kiosks. Be sure to punch in your ticket when boarding; random inspectors can land you with a fine even if you play the 'dumb' foreigner. Fares paid to the driver when boarding the bus are usually double the pre-purchase price.

Belgrade also has trams and trolleybuses with limited routes, while the bus system covers the whole city, even New Belgrade and the suburbs. Tram No 2 is useful for connecting the Kalemegdan Citadel with Trg Slavija, the bus station and the central train station.

Belgrade Bus Station. Tel: (011) 2627 146, 2622 526, 180 377 (international bus transport). Email: bas@bas.co.yu, saobracaj@bas.co.yu. www.bas.co.yu Transport Company 'Lasta'. Železnička 4 (Bus Station). Tel: (011) 688 515. Email: bgdbus@lasta.co.yu. www.lasta.co.yu

Serbia has a good bus service

Montenegro

Podgorica is the main bus hub for the country. There are daily buses to most Montenegrin destinations. The coastal area has an excellent bus service connecting all of the coastal cities. However, buses are known to be late and timetables occasionally inaccurate, so ask about times when purchasing your ticket.

Car hire

All the major cities in each country have car hire services, including the well-known Western car hire agencies. If you are planning a trip that involves several neighbouring countries, make sure you ask about cross-border regulations and insurance issues. You don't want to get to the border and have to pay extra insurance or not be able to enter the country at all.

Bosnia and Herzegovina

Hiring a car is very easy, but not entirely inexpensive. All major cities have car hire companies, and if you arrive at Sarajevo Airport, there are several rental places there and other agencies have airport pick-up. It's usually not a problem to hire a car without a reservation. Many of the major car hire agencies can be found via links from the international websites and through the international toll-free phone numbers.

Europcar. *Tel: (033) 289 273. Fax: (033) 460 737. Email: asa-rent@bih.net.ba*
Hertz. *Tel: (033) 668 186.*
Rent a Car SA. *Kranjčevićeva 39. Tel: (033) 219 177. Email: fracsa@team.ba. www.frac.co.ba*

Serbia

Car hire is often the best option for travelling long distances in Serbia, and it means that you can go at your own pace. With a good map, the roads are fairly easy to navigate, even though road conditions in some areas are poor at best. It is always advisable to search for guarded parking garages when leaving the car for any extended period of time.

Avis. *Bulevar Kralja Aleksandra 94, Belgrade. Tel: (011) 431 687, 433 314. Email: avis@eunet.yu. www.avis.co.yu*
Inex-co-Ineco. *Trg Republike 5/IX, Belgrade. Tel: (011) 620 980. Email: inecco@eunet.yu*

It's worth hiring a car in Serbia, when streets like these in Belgrade are easy to navigate

Putnik-Hertz. *Kneza Miloša 82, Belgrade. Tel: (011) 659 262, 641 566; Airport Belgrade. Tel: (011) 600 634.*
Unis. *Airport Belgrade. Tel: (011) 601 555, local 2754; Beogradska 71. Tel: (011) 3238 130.*

Montenegro

Car rental is available in the major cities of Budva, Bar, Podgorica, Ulcinj, Tivat, Herceg Novi, Kotor and Cetinje. You must be over 21 years old and have a valid driver's licence. Rates vary from agency to agency and according to the time of year. Drivers throughout the region are known to be slightly aggressive and fast.
Alliance. *Budva. Tel: (086) 452 753. Email: alliancebd@cg.yu. www.alliancetours.cg.yu*
Alliance. *Cetinje. Tel: (086) 231 157. www.alliancetours.cg.yu*

Europcar. *Podgorica. Tel: (069) 062 126. Email: adriaplus@cg.yu. www.europcar.com*
Forzza Cattaro. *Kotor. Tel: (082) 304 068.*
Kompas Hertz. *Ulcinj. Tel: (085) 313 597.*
Meridian. *Bar. Tel: (085) 314 000, 318 666. Email: meridian@cg.yu. www.meridian-rentacar.com*

By taxi

Taxis are a very efficient and affordable means of getting around all of the three countries, particularly in the larger cities. Rates are generally cheap, and taxi drivers are fair more often than not. Be sure they start the meter when you start your journey, and you can ask how much the journey will cost before you start.

Getting around

Road conditions can be very poor in parts of this region

Accommodation

A significant number of new hotels have been built in all three countries since 2000, and there are plans to greatly expand that capacity in the near future. Bosnia and Herzegovina has a limited selection outside the larger cities like Sarajevo and Mostar, but there are a good number of newer and smaller hotels that are often family-run. Outside Sarajevo there are no hostels to speak of.

Serbia has an increasing number of hotels and motels. Many of the socialist-style hotels still form the main accommodation in the smaller places, but the larger and more popular tourist destinations have a growing selection of good hotels.

Montenegro's Adriatic coast has a large accommodation capacity of all sorts. From seaside campsites, B&Bs, *pansions* and family-owned hotels to the larger hotel complexes, there is a good selection of affordable and comfortable places to stay.

The newer structures in Bosnia and Herzegovina, Serbia and Montenegro have many more creature comforts and are far better than the pre-war era socialist hotels that tend to lack style, hot water and comfort. Campsites are rather limited in the entire region, as is hostel accommodation. The smaller guesthouses or motels are often quite inexpensive and make great bargains for the mid-budget tourist. Luxury hotels are few and far between; there are only a handful of them in each country.

Bosnia and Herzegovina

Hotels and motels can be found in all towns and cities, and private rooms and apartments are also common throughout the country. A few hostels have opened in Bosnia and Herzegovina, namely in Sarajevo and Mostar. There are many *pansions* and B&Bs that are priced similarly to a western European hostel.

Sarajevo and Mostar have the best large hotels. When travelling elsewhere in the country, it's best to find a small hotel or motel. These are usually family-owned and operated, affordable and well kept. Although Mostar has the option of a larger hotel, the smaller *pansions* are great bargains and offer a full range of services with a much more homely atmosphere.

Serbia

Deluxe and A-class hotels are confined to Belgrade. The best hotels are always heavily booked, so advance reservations are essential. First-, second- and third-class *pansions* are available throughout the country. The larger hotels outside Belgrade and Novi Sad tend to be relics from the socialist era and don't always meet the tastes and requirements of Western travellers. It is best to seek out the small motels and *pansions* in the countryside, which are very modern and comfortable.

Montenegro

Montenegro has a wide variety of accommodation, ranging from modern, large and luxurious establishments to apartments and rooms in private houses. It is easy to find private accommodation – just look for signs with the word *sobe* (rooms). It is advisable to make advance bookings as the rooms go quickly in high season. Bookings can be made through a tourist agency or with the hotel directly. The information centres of the National Tourism Organisation of Montenegro are available to all visitors and can make bookings for you on the spot for hotels and B&Bs.

National Tourism Organisation of Montenegro, Rimski trg 10, Podgorica. Tel: (081) 235 155.
www.visit-montenegro.org

Dvori Balšića Hotel, Ulcinj

Food and drink

While each country and their respective regions have their own specialities, much of the traditional and national foods of Bosnia and Herzegovina, Serbia and Montenegro are the same, or, at the very least, similar in flavour and style. The western Balkan diet is based on meat dishes. The large rural areas that dominate all three countries have a long tradition of free-range, high-quality beef, lamb, pork and chicken. They take great pride in food preparation and pay close attention to where the livestock was raised and how the meat is cut. Thanks to the preservation of traditional rural lifestyles, most farmers raise their animals in an organic fashion.

Besides traditional and national food, there is a good Italian restaurant in most towns. Pizza and pasta are fairly popular. Continental food like *becka snicla* (Viennese schnitzel or veal medallion) can be found in most places as well. Asian food is rare, and Middle Eastern foods, like falafel or hummus, are almost non-existent except in Sarajevo.

Produce is mainly seasonal, and restaurants often serve what is available at that time of year. Fruit and vegetables are fresh and tasty, although not many places are particularly creative with their salads. There aren't a great number of cheeses to choose from, but the quality is exceptional, and the most popular are *kajmak* (cream cheese spread), *mladi sir* (young white cheese) and *travnicki* (a salty white cheese resembling feta).

Shopping for fresh food is always best at local open markets, which almost every town will have. The food is usually less expensive than in shops. The western Balkans still haven't completely bowed to the large supermarkets, and many small *prodavnica* (grocery stores) are family-owned and sell many of the products that the supermarkets do.

Fish is quite popular, and not just in the Mediterranean regions. On the coast and in Herzegovina, for obvious reasons, you can find excellent fresh seafood and shellfish. Inland, many restaurants serve trout, lake bass and carp. Trout from the fresh mountain rivers is excellent, and even the farmed trout are usually of good quality.

Vegetarians will have a tough time finding proper vegetarian dishes. You

SMOKING

Although the Western world is becoming more and more anti-smoking, with legal bans coming into force, be prepared to be overwhelmed by cigarette smoke in most places in the western Balkans. Not only does a high percentage of adults smoke, but most establishments have poor or no ventilation systems, and for some strange reason it just doesn't seem to bother them. During the summer months it's more bearable as the doors and windows are open. Clubs and bars, however, will be clouded in thick smoke. It is a rarity that someone will ask you if you 'mind' them smoking, and very common for people to light up at the dinner table even if others are still eating. You have been warned!

can always find food without meat, but it is usually a side dish like spinach, potatoes or carrots, or a pasta dish with tomato sauce. *Pita* is a filo-dough pastry dish made with cheese, spinach or potato and is a good lunch option. The coastal regions and the bigger cities are getting better at serving vegetarian food, but they are still a long way from vegetarian cuisine culture.

Drinking is not taken lightly here. Spirits are quite common throughout the entire region. In the continental, alpine climates, *rakija* (plum brandy) is by far the most popular choice of hard alcohol. *Jabukovaca* (apple brandy) and *kruske* (pear brandy) are also homemade specialities found in most traditional restaurants. The coastal regions drink a brandy made from grape called *loza*, which is very similar to Italian *grappa*.

Wine and beer are widely drunk in restaurants, bars and clubs. Herzegovina and Montenegro make the best red wines, and some of the better white wines in the region come from the Fruška Gora area. Montenegro's Vranac red is very popular, as is Blatina from Herzegovina. All bars and most restaurants serve the classic drinks and cocktails made from gin, whisky and vodka.

Tipping in restaurants is normal and the usual rate is about 10 per cent, not more. In cafés and bars, there isn't much of a tradition of tipping, but for good service tipping is always welcome.

Bosnia and Herzegovina specialities

Bamija – okra with veal.
Begova Čorba – the most popular soup, made of veal and vegetables.
Čevapi – small meat sausages of lamb and beef mix. These are usually served with fresh onions and *pita* bread on the side. *Čevapi* usually come in pointed finger-size sausages and are offered in five or ten pieces.
Sitni cevap – small beef bits in a thick carrot stew.
Sogandolma – fried onions stuffed with minced meat.

Wines

Sharing a similar climate and topsoil with Dalmatia, the savoury reds

Food and drink

and dry whites of Herzegovina can easily compare to some of Croatia's finest. Ask for domestic wines like Stankela, Gangas, Andrija and Vukovic.

Serbian specialities

Grah s suvim mesom – bean stew.
Hajducki rostilj – 'rebels' mixed meat grill.
Karadjordje – steak.
Kuvani kupus – stewed sauerkraut.
Kupus s jaretina – cabbage with mutton.

Wines and spirits

Try the 'tea of Šumadija' (tea of the foresters) – a boiled brandy. The cellars of Sremski Karlovci, Vršac, Župa and Smederevo region hold Serbia's best wines.

Montenegrin specialities

Pljevaljski sir – cheese from Pljevlja.
Njeguški pršut – smoked ham.
Njeguški sir – cheese.

Northern region specialities

Cicvara – buttered corn porridge.
Janjetina kuhana u mlijeku – lamb cooked in milk.
Kuhana janjetina – boiled lamb.
Kuhani krompiri sa sirom i vrhnjem – boiled potatoes with cheese and fresh cream.

Central and coastal areas

A selection of traditional recipes from the central and coastal areas will

COMMON TRADITIONAL DISHES

Burek – a meat pie.
Filovane paprike – fried peppers stuffed with minced meat and spices.
Ispod sača – meals baked in a 'Dutch oven' (*ispod sača*) or a metal pan covered in hot ash.
Jagnjetina – lamb grilled over an open fire.
Krompiruša – diced potatoes with spices.
Lonac – meat and vegetable stew cooked over an open fire.
Musaka – a meat pie made of minced beef, very similar to cottage pie.
Pita – filo-dough pastry with various fillings.
Pršut – air-dried or smoked ham, similar to Italian prosciutto.
Rostilj – grill. In all regions of the western Balkans grilling meat is very popular.
Sarme – meat and rice rolled in cabbage or grape leaves.
Sirnica – made from a fresh, homemade cheese.
Sudžuk – beef sausages with a similar form to pepperoni, very popular in Bosnia.
Suho meso – dried meat, either beef or pork.
Teletina – veal, usually served in cutlets (*ispod sača*). Veal in the Balkans is free range.
Zeljanica – made from spinach and cheese.

include *Kastradina* (dried mutton) and smoked and fresh carp (from Lake Skadar).

Wine

The best-known Montenegrin wines are the premium Vranac, Pro Corde, Krstač, Cabernet, Chardonnay and the famous homemade Crmničko red wine.

Sauvignon blanc wine grapes grown in Vlasotince vineyards, southeast Serbia

Entertainment

Entertainment can, of course, come in many forms. There is a significant difference in the definition of entertainment between rural and urban areas. The best museums, festivals and concerts take place in Sarajevo, Belgrade and Novi Sad, but live music can be found almost anywhere. Although the partying and clubbing culture is on the rise, café culture still very much dominates entertainment circles. Cafés will be teeming day and night in most places that you go, and many transform into nightclubs later in the evening. Outdoor sports – both on the coast and inland – are becoming more readily accessible to foreign guests. Hiking, skiing, rafting and watersports are offered throughout the region. It's always best to ask at your hotel or at an information centre about when and where the various types of entertainment may be occurring.

Bars

Bars are much more common than pubs. Many daytime cafés turn into bars and even clubs at night. In the high season, bars are very crowded and smoky, with music so loud that you may have to shout to be heard. Alcohol is very reasonably priced. Bars often have DJs on weekends and occasional live music concerts. *Bars stay open late, often into the morning on weekends.*

Cafés

The entire western Balkans has an amazing café culture. Cafés are as common here as pubs are in the UK, and they are almost always packed with people. This obsession with coffee keeps prices down, and excellent cafés serve all sorts of coffee at a fraction of Western European prices. Most cafés serve the standard espresso, cappuccino, and a latte or something similar.

In many rural areas, only Turkish coffee is served – this is prepared differently from place to place. Sarajevo's version of Turkish coffee is by far the best. Served in a Turkish-style coffee set and with Turkish delight, it's a delicious and strong coffee mostly sipped in the old town. The Serbs will serve Turkish coffee in a regular coffee cup – when ordering you are expected to indicate whether or not you want sugar. Be careful because at the bottom of the cup there will be a thick layer of coffee grinds. Local people very often ask friends or new acquaintances for a coffee; it is common practice that the one who invited you pays the bill. Tipping isn't expected in most cafés.

Cafés are open from early morning until around 11pm.

Cinema

The former Yugoslavia has a fantastic film industry. Unfortunately, most of the locally produced films can be seen with English subtitles only at film fests or on DVD. Only the bigger cities have cinemas, and you should enquire about English-language subtitles. English-language films are usually left in English and have Serbian/Bosnian/Croatian subtitles. Entrance fees are reasonable.

Folk music

Folk music is extremely popular in the western Balkans. There is a new movement of 'turbo folk' which is not well liked by most foreigners. The old, authentic folk music is a little harder to find, but it won't disappoint you. Some traditional restaurants have folk bands playing at weekends.

The Guča Trumpet Festival in August is a marvellous collection of gypsy and local folk music (*see p19*). Sarajevo also has an international folk music festival in October. Contact the tourist information centres for information.

Interacting with the locals

Spanning all generations, cafés are by far the most popular pastime in the western Balkans. All cities and towns will have walking promenades lined with cafés, and most people stroll with

A typical street café in Belgrade

friends and stop at a café or two for a drink or a snack. The younger generations also entertain themselves at bars and clubs, whereas restaurants are more popular with the slightly older crowds. Locals love to sing and dance and spontaneous sing-alongs to popular songs (especially from the Yugoslav days) are common. The theatre, opera and ballet crowds are only found in the major cities; although they are a considerably smaller group, the quality of the performing arts in this region is quite high.

Live music

The big cities have live music venues, and most of the music is of a local character. Bars or clubs usually have rock bands, and a few places in Belgrade, Novi Sad and Sarajevo play

Sarajevo jazz festival

live jazz regularly. The EXIT Festival in Novi Sad is the very best live music show in southeast Europe (*see pp60–61*). Vrnjačka Banja is famous for its live local music that is played in most traditional restaurants in town. On the coast during the high season, there are regular concerts and several music festivals, with the highlight of Songs of the Mediterranean in July. Live music, especially local bands, is not always easy to find or well marketed in English – ask at the tourist information centres where good live music can be found.

Pubs

Pubs are a little less common in the western Balkans than in the rest of Europe. Like anywhere in Europe these days, there will always be an Irish pub in the bigger towns that serves local beer on tap and usually a few imports. The pubs tend to mostly attract younger crowds in their twenties and thirties, and all pubs play modern and mostly Western music. There are often pool tables as well. Local beer is generally quite cheap, and the classic imports like Heineken, Amstel and Stella Artois are usually double the price.
Pubs stay open until midnight on average.

Restaurants

Many traditional restaurants often have live music, some of it quite good although at times it doesn't seem to appeal to Western tastes. People tend to take long dinners with friends and family, and a significant amount of drinking is commonplace. Casual dress is the norm in most restaurants and very few establishments have a dress code.

Restaurants stay open from around 10am to midnight.

Theatre

The best theatre is found in Belgrade, Sarajevo and Novi Sad. Most productions, with the exception of a few international theatre festivals, are performed in the local language. If you are a theatre fan, then that might not matter. MESS alternative theatre festival in Sarajevo (*see p19*) hosts a wide range of international performances. Theatre tickets are affordable but for major productions they are often sold out before the day of the event. Tickets are sold at the venue's box office.

Tourist attractions

Many of the new local tour packages offer entertainment content in their arrangements such as folk music or a folk dance. The festivals, particularly in Belgrade, Sarajevo and Novi Sad, have had more of an international slant to them in recent years, with great programmes in both English and the local language.

Serbian National Theatre, Novi Sad

Shopping

The best kind of shopping to do in any country is the kind that supports local communities. Traditional handicrafts are still produced in most areas of the western Balkans, and they provide vital economic assistance to many of the rural areas in the region.

There are duty-free shops at all of the airports in the tri-country region. None of the countries are in the EU, and so there are duty-free alcohol, cigarettes, perfumes and chocolates available. The standard limit is 200 cigarettes and 2 litres of alcohol.

Bosnia and Herzegovina

Bosnia and Herzegovina is known for many ancient handicrafts. During the Ottoman era, places like Sarajevo, Mostar, Travnik, Konjic and Visoko became well known for their skilled coppersmiths, leather-smiths, gold- and

Souvenirs in the Bascarsija District, Sarajevo

Rugs for sale in Mostar

silversmiths, as well as their skilled wood-carvers. This tradition has been passed on from generation to generation and still thrives today. These old crafts, known as *stari zanati*, are practised in the old Turkish quarters of all of the above-mentioned towns.

Sarajevo and Mostar are the only locations featured in this guide with brand-name boutiques. Both cities have several large shopping centres, albeit out of the old towns.

Sarajevo's Baščaršija and Ferhadija walkway are the best shopping areas in town. A classic gift from Sarajevo is the copper tea and coffee sets sold on Kazandziluk Street in the old town. They are very well made, easy to travel with, and can be used practically or as a decoration. Many shops in the old

town will also sell hand-woven carpets with old Bosnian motifs and styles. The gold and silver jewellery is usually less expensive than in Western countries and the craftsmanship is very good.

Mostar is well known for its coppersmiths and lovely carvings of the old bridge (Stari Most), pomegranates or the ancient symbols from the medieval tombstones. The art galleries along both sides of the Stari Most sell a wide range of the beautiful paintings of the trademark bridge.

Visoko, quickly becoming popular for its supposed pyramids, has long been known for its high-quality leather products. In the old town markets as well as on the roadsides, everything from pilot jackets to handmade leather carpets is on sale.

Travnik, situated just below Vlasic Mountain, is famous for its highland shepherd cultures and sells a wide range of colourful wool products made by the village women. In the town of Konjic, where the white-water rafting companies for the Neretva are located, the Niksic family – originally from Montenegro – has a long tradition of producing the country's finest intricate Ottoman wood carvings. Ottoman-style tables and tiny chairs are very popular with both locals and tourists.

It is always a good idea to purchase locally made goods. Bosnia and Herzegovina is a country still experiencing a difficult economic and social transformation. A direct economic stimulus will help these communities get back on their feet.

Serbia

In Belgrade, the Knez Mihailova pedestrian zone, extending from Trg Republike to Kalemegdan, is the main shopping area. There you can find most of the high-street names and brands as well as local artisans and craftspeople selling their wares. No less popular is the area around Terazije Square. This stretch of shops offers a wide variety of clothes outlets.

For quality 'ethno' souvenirs, visit the Ethnographic Museum shop (*Etno dućan, Studentski Trg 13*). For film-lovers, there are copies of all of Emir

Bosnian coppersmith's have passed down their skills since the 15th century

Kusturica's films on sale in the city, but make sure they are subtitled in English.

Souvenir shops

Etno dućan *Studentski Trg 13. Tel: (011) 3281 888.*
Etno magazine Gral *Zetska 13. Tel: (011) 3246 583.*
Flowers and Arts *Kosančićev Venac 5. Tel: (011) 638 257.*
NARODNA Radinost *Zeleni venac. Tel: (011) 631 423.*

Around Novi Sad and Fruška Gora, you can find several good purchases, namely the locally made wines and spirits and the handmade souvenirs available in many of the Serbian Orthodox monasteries. In the rural areas of Fruška Gora, there are many handicrafts sold by the local villagers, from wool socks to small wood carvings. The same goes for southern Serbia. The rural and mountain areas are famous for their wool products of all types. Some of these regions, particularly around the Zlatibor area, are also well known for wood carvings. The best brandy (*rakija*) in the wider region is a plum brandy called Slijivovica, from southwest Serbia.

Montenegro

For high-street shopping with brand-name shops, Podgorica, Budva, Kotor and Sveti Stefan are the places to go. New shopping centres are found in the larger towns, and are usually located out of the centre. All of the coastal towns have a nice selection of locally made souvenirs. You may have to look a little harder for authentic handmade goods, but most of the workshops are found in the old towns.

Many of the Orthodox monasteries sell beautiful handmade souvenirs. Some also sell wine or cheese produced by the monks themselves. Ostrog Monastery near Niksic (*see p90*) has lovely Christian paintings and icons. The souvenir shop at Njegoš' mausoleum on Lovćen also sells many Orthodox and Montenegrin souvenirs (*see p82*). The northern areas have a largely rural population, and their traditional lifestyles include the handmade production of wool and wood products. Wool socks, jumpers and hats are quite commonly sold in the mountainous north; the wool may be a bit rough but if it keeps the locals warm, it will keep you warm too.

A nice gift from Montenegro is a few bottles of its red wines, like Vranac and Pro Corde, and local spirits. More and more shops are catching on to the popularity of Montenegrin alcohol and they sell gift packages for tourists.

Town markets sell fresh fruit and vegetables, cheese, meat and fish, as well as cheap clothing and household goods.

Shops. Open: Mon–Fri 9am–9pm, Sat 8am–3pm (many shops open all day Sat). Shops in tourist resorts often stay open until midnight in the high season. Grocery stores. Open: 6am–10pm.

Sport and leisure

Each country offers a vast range of activities, from adventure to relaxation, on both land and water. Hiking and trekking are popular activities in the national parks, and whitewater rafting is a well-developed adventure sport in Bosnia and Herzegovina and Montenegro.

Bosnia and Herzegovina

Biking

The highlands of the Bosnian part of the Central Dinaric Alps have a well-developed trail system designed by the Mountain Bike Association of Bosnia and Herzegovina and Ciclo Centar from Sarajevo. They offer full gear rental, guides, and maps on some of the best mountain-bike trails in Europe (*see p158*).

Cross-country skiing through Bosnia's pine

Hiking

Hiking the mountains of Bosnia and Herzegovina is definitely one of the best ways to get some exercise and to catch a few unforgettable views of the highland villages. Green Visions (*see p159*) is the only eco-tourism group in Sarajevo organising daily hikes around Sarajevo from April to October; they do snowshoe treks in the winter months as well.

Horse-riding

The major centre for horse-riding near Sarajevo is in Rogatica just outside of Sarajevo. This is a French-run horse farm that offers riding to adults and children. The rates are very affordable. *Borike Horse Farm, 18km (11 miles) from Rogatica. Tel: (058) 410 925.*

Rafting

Bosnia and Herzegovina is well known for its white-water rafting adventures, and this is by far the best-developed

Rafting on the Neretva River

outdoor activity. Bosnia has four raging rivers that have professionally guided rafting tours (*see pp152 & 153*). The Neretva, Vrbas, Una and Tara rivers rank among Europe's best, and you'll be pleasantly surprised by the pristine wilderness that accompanies the ride.

Skiing

For winter guests there are, of course, the Olympic ski mountains of Jahorina and Bjelašnica. These were the locations for the 14th Winter Olympic Games and offer the best and most affordable skiing in southeast Europe – Olympic-quality skiing for just a fraction of the cost of Western European ski centres.

Serbia
Fishing

Fly and sport fishing is very popular in Serbia. The Danube and Sava rivers are popular fishing spots, but the truly great fishing in Serbia is in the southwestern regions on the Drina River and the other mountain rivers and lakes that are abundant in fish. Fishing permits are available from hotels or local authorities.

Golf

The small BeogradAda golf course isn't exactly St Andrews but if you want to swing the clubs, this is the best place to do it.
Ciganlija 2, Belgrade. Tel: (011) 3346 824. www.golfclub.co.yu

Hiking

The hiking and walking in the Kopaonik and Zlatibor areas and Tara National Park are the country's best. For great village and country walking, Fruška Gora National Park near Novi Sad has organised walks through tour operators and the Mountain Association has hikes every Sunday.

Skiing

The best ski centres in the country are at Kopaonik, where there are proper facilities and lifts. Zlatibor has a smaller piste with a lift for recreational skiing.

Thermal spas

Vrnjačka Banja is Serbia's famous spa area, with six major thermal spas (*see p66*). There are full facilities available,

from massage and jacuzzi to medical treatment for ailments.

Montenegro
Boating

There are many opportunities for fun and relaxing boat rides in Montenegro. The Bay of Kotor has a lovely day trip to the islands. From Budva, there are ferry boats to St Nikola island. On Lake Skadar, a little inland, there are great boat rides through the lake system and opportunities for bird-watching.

Hiking

The northern territories are Montenegro's best hiking grounds. Both Biogradska National Park and Durmitor National Park (*see pp105 & 106*) have a great system of hiking trails that covers hundreds of

Scuba diving near Ulcinj

Windsurfing in Ada Bojana

kilometres of phenomenal mountain terrain. Lovćen National Park near Cetinje also has nice walking trails (*see p108*).

Rafting

Europe's deepest canyon provides the best rafting event in southeast Europe. The Tara River Canyon is visited by tens of thousands of nature and rafting enthusiasts, and there are one- to three-day rafting adventures available. Most tour operators on the coast offer Tara rafting trips.
Tara Tour, Plužine. Tel: (083) 271 359. www.tara-tour.com

Sailing

Sailing is available with some of the region's best skippers. If you know your way around a sailing boat, rentals are possible but rather

expensive. Budva has sailing boat rentals and sailing rides (ask the tourism information centre for more details).

Skiing

Durmitor National Park hosts the country's largest ski centre. The facilities are a little old but there is good skiing in an amazing mountain landscape. The ski centre on Zabljak has accommodation and full gear rental.

Watersports

Montenegro's coast has greatly improved its water sport agenda in the past few years. With Budva, Ulcinj and Ada Bojana as the main centres, diving, windsurfing, jet ski rides and snorkelling are offered with full gear rental, training and safety equipment.

Children

The entire former Yugoslavia is very child friendly. Children are welcome in restaurants and cafés with few exceptions. In fact, most cafés and restaurants go out of their way to provide special orders for children, but not many areas are specifically designed for children.

Bosnia and Herzegovina

Lutkarsko Kazalište Mostar

Children's puppet theatre in Mostar.
Trg Hrvatskih Velikana bb. Tel/Fax: (036) 314 893. Email: lutkari@lutkamo.org

Sarajevo Zoo

The zoo does not have many exotic animals, but it is a great place for children with a large playground and feeding zoo section.
Patriotske Lige.

Terme Ilidža

There are excellent swimming facilities for children here, and the Vrelo Bosne Park in Ilidža is a wonderful place for children to run around and play.
Mala Aleja 40 (behind Dom Zdravlje), Ilidža. Tel: (033) 771 011. Fax: (033) 771 010. Email: info@terme-catez.si. www.terme-ilidza.ba. Swimming pool open: 9am–9pm. Admission charge. Tropical garden open: 8am–10pm. Restaurant open: 8.30am–10.30pm.

Serbia

Belgrade Zoo

Situated at the very centre of the city, the Belgrade Zoo stands on one of the most attractive city locations – the Kalemegdan Park.
Mali Kalemegdan 8, Belgrade. Tel: (011) 624 526. Open: 8am–5pm (winter); 8am–8.30pm (summer). www.beozoovrt.izlog.org

There are some great beaches for kids around Budva

Pan Theatre

Belgrade's little theatre has a wide repertoire for children.
Bulevar Kralja Aleksandra 298, Belgrade. Tel: (011) 3472 984. www.panteatar.co.yu

Montenegro

There are no children's facilities such as theatres or zoos in Montenegro.

Most of the children's activities are based on the beach and watersports. There are paddle boats and other fun rides for kids on several beaches, including Budva and Ada Bojana (*see p74 & p85*). Many of the larger hotels have swimming pools, and during the high season organise activities for kids.

Sightseeing in Mostar before checking out the puppet theatre

Essentials

ARRIVING
By air
Bosnia and Herzegovina

Sarajevo is well connected with direct British Airways flights from Gatwick, London. There are also direct flights from Zagreb, Vienna, Frankfurt, Milan, Ljubljana, Budapest, Munich, Belgrade and Istanbul. Sarajevo International Airport has a comprehensive list of all scheduled flights. *Sarajevo International Airport. Kurta Schorka 36. Tel: (033) 289 121, 289 100. www.sarajevo-airport.ba*

Serbia

Jat Airways is the national carrier of Serbia. It has direct or linked flights to most major European cities flying into Belgrade and the southern city of Niš. *Jat Airways. Bulevar Umetnosti 16. Tel: (011) 3114 222. Fax: (011) 3112 853. www.jat.com*

Montenegro

Montenegro Airlines, in cooperation with Austria Airlines, has several linked flights to Frankfurt, Vienna, Zurich, Paris, Budapest, Bari, Rome, Ljubljana and Belgrade. During the summer season, there are charter flights from abroad to the airports of Tivat and Podgorica. *Montenegro Airlines. Podgorica Slobode 23. Tel: (081) 664 411, 664 433; booking: 9804. www.montenegro-airlines.cg.yu*

By sea
Bosnia and Herzegovina

As Bosnia and Herzegovina has only about 24km (15 miles) of coast, at Neum, no ferries dock here. The ports of Split and Dubrovnik, however, are very popular and are an efficient means of transport from Italy (Ancona and Bari respectively). The bus station in Split is at the port, making the transfer easy and hassle-free. Dubrovnik's bus station is also near the port, but it does not have the same volume of traffic as Split. Nonetheless, there are several weekly ferries from Bari, on the southeastern coast of Italy. The ferry schedules vary depending on the season. Ferries from Ancona to

Dubrovnik port

Split and Bari to Dubrovnik can be found on the websites of these companies: SEM (*www.sem-marina.hr*), Jadrolinija (*www.jadrolinija.hr*) and Adriatica Navigazione (*www.adriatica.it*).

Serbia

Belgrade has a commercial port on the banks of the River Danube called Luka Beograd. There is also a tourist port on the banks of the River Sava welcoming various river cruise vessels from across Europe.
Port of Belgrade. Tel: (011) 752 971. www.port-bgd.co.yu

Montenegro

The coast of the Adriatic Sea makes Montenegro accessible by boat, yacht, ferry and cruiser. There are several passenger ferry companies operating regular connections between Montenegro and Italy. Ships sail on lines between Bar–Bari, Bar–Ancona and Kotor–Bari. During the summer months, the frequency of lines is increased. The port of Bar is the biggest port in Montenegro.
Port of Bar. Tel: (085) 312 366. www.lukabar.cg.yu

Kotor Ferry Service

You can save some time by taking the Lepetani–Kamenari car ferry at Verige (the narrowest part of the Bay of Kotor) instead of driving all the way around the Bay of Kotor.
The terminals are Kamenari – 12km

Sarajevo's modern city centre

(7¹/₂ miles) from the town of Herceg Novi – and Lepetani.
The ferry runs regularly and operates 30 Sept–1 June 5am–midnight & 1 June–30 Sept 24 hours. Tel: (088) 673 558. For more detailed information, refer to the official website of the National Tourism Organisation of Montenegro, www.visit-montenegro.org

By rail
Bosnia and Herzegovina

Trains to Bosnia and Herzegovina all travel through Croatia and Hungary. From the Dalmatian coast town of Ploče, there are daily trains via Mostar to Sarajevo. Sarajevo is connected with daily direct trains to both Zagreb and Budapest.
Sarajevo railway station. Tel: (033) 657 313.

Serbia

Rail services to Belgrade run from Bulgaria, Budapest, Croatia, Greece, Montenegro, Romania, Russia and Turkey. Trains from Western Europe travel via Budapest.

For up-to-date information, contact:
Rail Europe. Tel: 08705 848 848.
www.raileurope.co.uk
Railway Enterprise 'Belgrade'.
Nemanjina 6. Tel: (011) 361 4811/6722.
Email: posta@yurail.co.yu.
www.yurail.co.yu

Montenegro

The only way to Montenegro by rail is via Belgrade. Serbia's capital city is well connected to regional hubs, and Budapest acts as the main connection point for trains from Western Europe.

www.zeljeznica.cg.yu

By bus
Bosnia and Herzegovina

The main bus operator in Bosnia and Herzegovina is called Centrotrans, and almost every bus connection can be made through it. It works with the main European bus operators, including Eurolines. Bus schedules, online reservations and main European office addresses can be found on the website (*www.centrotrans.com*).

Serbia

Regular and seasonal international bus lines link Serbia to most European countries. The international bus lines to Western Europe mainly focus on Germany and Austria, where buses can be taken for all other destinations.

Srbija tours international. Lička 3.
Belgrade. Tel: (011) 3614 545. Open:

A city bus in Novi Sad

Essentials

Mon–Fri 8am–7pm, Sat 8am–6pm, Sun 8am–1pm. www.srbija-tours.com

Montenegro

Montenegro has regular bus services from Croatia, Bosnia and Herzegovina, Serbia, Austria and Germany. If travelling in the region, there are direct bus services from Dubrovnik, Sarajevo and Belgrade to both Podgorica and the coastal areas.

www.tourism-montenegro.com

Serbian currency: Dinar

By car

Travelling by car to any of these destinations is feasible via Croatia or Hungary. With regular EU insurance and vehicle registration, there is no problem for a car to enter and freely travel in the western Balkans. Speed limits vary but are well posted. Wearing of seat belts is compulsory.

Customs

Customs in all three countries are fairly lax towards Western travellers. You are limited to 200 cigarettes and 2 litres of alcohol. You are discouraged from bringing fruits or meats in from other countries, but controls on these items are almost non-existent. Trying to get tax rebates is quite complicated and often not worth the hassle. Customs officials have the right to search all of your belongings at the border and will do so occasionally.

Departing

Departure from any of these three countries is relatively straightforward. Whether travelling by aeroplane, car, ferry or train, customs and border control are usually quite expedient and carry out routine checks of passports. Make sure you confirm your reservations for trains, planes and ferries because they are known, on occasion, to overbook or cancel a scheduled journey and not let passengers know. Choose your travel routes by car or bus carefully to avoid areas with a lot of congestion. The Croatian coast in the summertime is a nightmare for traffic; it's often better to travel on smaller roads or on Serbia's major motorway to avoid a wait.

Electricity

The western Balkan nations use 220 volts and the standard continental European two-pin plugs. It is difficult to find adaptors for UK or US plugs, so buy one before you arrive.

Money

ATMs (cash machines) can be found in the larger towns in all the countries or on the coast in Montenegro. All banks will exchange currency at more or less the same rate. It is not recommended to change money on the street as counterfeit currency is present in the region. Credit card use is gaining wider acceptance, but is still quite limited even in the capital cities. Be sure to ask if you want to pay with a credit card.

Bosnia and Herzegovina

The official currency in Bosnia and Herzegovina is the konvertebilna marka (KM), which is also abbreviated to BAM. Euros are widely accepted in most places except public institutions such as the post office, etc.

Serbia

The official currency in Serbia is the New Yugoslav Dinar (CSD). One New Yugoslav Dinar is equal to 100 paras. Notes are in denominations of CSD 10, 20, 50, 100, 200, 1,000 and 5,000. Coins are in denominations of CSD 2, 5, 10 and 20, and 1 and 50 paras. The euro and dollar are preferred currencies to exchange or use.

Montenegro

Montenegro's official currency is the euro and notes are issued in denominations of 5, 10, 20, 50, 100, 200 and 500 euros. Coins are issued in denominations of 1, 2, 5, 10, 20 and 50 cents and 1 and 2 euros.

Opening hours

Most shops are open Monday to Saturday from 8am–8pm. During the high season (July and August), many shops will remain open until 10pm, especially in the old towns. Food stores and supermarkets are open until 10pm. There are several 24-hour shops that are marked '0–24'. Open-air markets usually open a little earlier at 7am and only close at nightfall in the summer months, but officially at 7pm. Banks are generally open from 8am–8pm. Public institutions close rather early, some at 3pm but most at 4pm.

Passports and visas
Bosnia and Herzegovina

For holders of valid passports from all EU countries, the USA, Canada and New Zealand, no visa is required for stays up to 90 days. Holders of Australian passports must obtain visas at the Bosnian embassy (*5 Beale Crescent, Deakin ACT 2600. Tel: (02) 6232 4646*). Visa applications usually take three weeks to process because all applications are sent to and verified in Sarajevo. For any further information, contact the Embassy of Bosnia and Herzegovina in the UK (*5–7 Lexham Gardens, London W8 5JJ. Tel: (020) 7373 0867. Open: Mon–Fri 9am–5pm, Sat 10am–1pm*).

Serbia

For EU, Australian, Canadian or US citizens, only a valid passport is necessary for entry. Citizens of these countries don't need a visa or return ticket. All other countries should check with the Ministry of Foreign Affairs of Serbia (*Kneza Miloša 24–26. Tel: (011) 3615 666/055. Fax: (011) 3618 366. www.mfa.gov.yu*).

Montenegro

Citizens of all EU countries, the USA, Canada, Australia and New Zealand do not need an entry visa for a visit of up to 30 days but they do need a valid passport. South African citizens need a visa. All necessary documentation information for travelling to Montenegro can be found at the Ministry of Foreign Affairs of Montenegro (*Tel: (081) 224 609, 246 357. Email: mip@cg.yu. www.mip.cg.yu*).

Pharmacies

Pharmacies are called *apoteka* in the local language. They are quite modern in most places, and larger towns will always have a 24-hour pharmacy for emergencies. Pharmacies sell over-the-counter drugs as well as some prescription drugs, and they are all staffed with professional pharmacists.

Post offices

Stamps (*marka*; plural *marke*) can only be bought at a post office. The post within Europe takes approximately a week and usually around two weeks to the USA. The post office is unpredictable with its delivery timing, and sending packages to any destination is quite expensive,

Essentials

CONVERSION TABLE

FROM	TO	MULTIPLY BY
Inches	Centimetres	2.54
Feet	Metres	0.3048
Yards	Metres	0.9144
Miles	Kilometres	1.6090
Acres	Hectares	0.4047
Gallons	Litres	4.5460
Ounces	Grams	28.35
Pounds	Grams	453.6
Pounds	Kilograms	0.4536
Tons	Tonnes	1.0160

To convert back, for example from centimetres to inches, divide by the number in the third column.

MEN'S SUITS

UK		36	38	40	42	44	46	48
Bosnia, Serbia & Montenegro and Rest of Europe		46	48	50	52	54	56	58
USA		36	38	40	42	44	46	48

DRESS SIZES

UK	8	10	12	14	16	18
France	36	38	40	42	44	46
Italy	38	40	42	44	46	48
Bosnia, Serbia & Montenegro and Rest of Europe	34	36	38	40	42	44
USA	6	8	10	12	14	16

MEN'S SHIRTS

UK	14	14.5	15	15.5	16	16.5	17
Bosnia, Serbia & Montenegro and Rest of Europe	36	37	38	39/40	41	42	43
USA	14	14.5	15	15.5	16	16.5	17

MEN'S SHOES

UK	7	7.5	8.5	9.5	10.5	11
Bosnia, Serbia & Montenegro and Rest of Europe	41	42	43	44	45	46
USA	8	8.5	9.5	10.5	11.5	12

WOMEN'S SHOES

UK	4.5	5	5.5	6	6.5	7
Bosnia, Serbia & Montenegro and Rest of Europe	38	38	39	39	40	41
USA	6	6.5	7	7.5	8	8.5

including using any of the Western couriers like DHL or Fedex.

Public holidays

Bosnia and Herzegovina

1 Jan – Catholic New Year
7 Jan – Orthodox Christmas
14 Jan – Orthodox New Year
1 Mar – Independence Day
1 May – Labour Day
25 Dec – Catholic Christmas
Islamic – Ramadan Bajram
Kurban Bajram (Muslim Holy Day) – The date for this holiday is related to moon cycles and is not the same every year, so can be celebrated up to three days later.

Serbia

1 Jan – New Year's Day
7 Jan – Orthodox Christmas Day
15 Feb – Serbia National Day
6 Apr – Orthodox Good Friday
8 Apr – Orthodox Easter
27 Apr – Constitution Day
1 May – May Day

Montenegro

1 Jan – New Year's Day (two days)
6 Jan – Orthodox Christmas Eve
7 Jan – Orthodox Christmas Day
8 Jan – Second Day of Orthodox Christmas
6 Apr – Orthodox Good Friday
8 Apr – Orthodox Easter
9 Apr – Orthodox Easter Monday
27 Apr – Constitution Day
1 May – May Day
13 July – Revolution Day

Islamic – Ramadan Bayram
Kurban Bayram

Sustainable tourism

Thomas Cook is a strong advocate of ethical and fairly traded tourism and believes that the travel experience should be as good for the places visited as it is for the people who visit them. That's why we firmly support The Travel Foundation, a charity that develops solutions to help improve and protect holiday destinations, their environment, traditions and culture. To find out what you can do to make a positive difference to the places you travel to and the people who live there, please visit *www.thetravelfoundation.org.uk*

Telephone

Mobile phone use in the western Balkans is extremely popular. It is very expensive to use a roaming service in this region and it may be wiser to buy a local SIM card that you can use in the region. There are mobile service centres everywhere, but for a new SIM card you must go to a post office or official branch of the service provider. Telephone booths and call centres (usually at the post office) both have good connections and are not terribly expensive. Telephone cards can be bought at kiosks in towns everywhere.

Email and internet

Internet use is quickly spreading throughout the region. Many hotels and *pansions* have picked up on the demand for internet connections and many have installed them. There are internet cafés in cities and towns throughout the entire region.

Time zones

Bosnia, Herzegovina and Serbia & Montenegro are on Central European Time (CET). They are one hour ahead of GMT; six hours ahead of Eastern Time (ET); nine ahead of Pacific Time (PT); eight hours behind Sydney, Australia; and ten behind New Zealand.

Toilets

Most places in the western Balkans do not require you to be a customer in order to use their toilet facilities. It is best to ask, but it is a rarity for a foreigner to be rejected. Toilets are almost exclusively labelled 'WC' or 'Toilet'. The women's toilet will be labelled 'Ž' for *ženski* (female) and the men's 'M' for *muški* (male). In many of the older buildings, the toilet will simply be a hole in the ground, usually with no toilet paper. Look for newer establishments for modern facilities. A few places will charge for using the toilet and public toilets are not very common.

Travellers with disabilities

Assistance or facilities for people with disabilities is practically non-existent in the western Balkans. Some cities may have installed ramps for wheelchairs, but this is not always consistent throughout the city. Expect to have a difficult time if you are a traveller with a disability.

Essentials

Be respectful of the countryside when out and about

Language

The languages used in Bosnia and Herzegovina, Serbia and Montenegro are basically one and the same. The languages may have different names, but the differences are strictly those of dialect, similar to the English of the USA, UK and Australia. The old name for the language was Serbo-Croat and this has now been divided into Serbian, Bosnian and Croatian.

English is widely spoken in the urban areas, particularly by the younger generations. German is also a common second language among the local people.

English	Bosnian	Approx pronunciation
BASICS		
Yes	Da	*Dah*
No	Ne	*Neh*
Please	Molim	*Moh-leem*
Thank you	Hvala lijepo	*Hvah-lah lee-yeh-poh*
Hello	Dobar dan	*Doh-bahr dahn*
Goodbye	Do viđenja	*Doh vee-jeh-nyah*
Excuse me	Oprostite	*Oh-prohs-tee-teh*
Sorry	Izvinite	*Eez-vee-nee-teh*
That's okay	Uredu je	*oo-reh-doo-yeh*
To	do	*dough*
From	od	*ohd*
I don't understand	Ne razumijem	*Neh rah-zoo-mee-yehn*
Do you speak English?	Da li govorite engleski?	*Dah-lee goh-voh-ree-the ehn-glehskee?*
Good morning	Dobro jutro	*Doh-broh yoo-troh*
Good afternoon	Dobar dan	*Doh-bar-dahn*
Good evening	Dobro većer	*Doh-broh veh-chehr*
Goodnight	Laku noć	*Lah-koo nohtch*
My name is ...	Zovem se ...	*Zoh-vehm seh ...*
DAYS & TIMES		
Monday	Ponedjeljak	*Poh-ned-yeh-lyak*
Tuesday	Utorak	*Ootorak*
Wednesday	Srijeda	*Sreeyeda*
Thursday	Četvrtak	*Chetvrtak*
Friday	Petak	*Peh-tak*
Saturday	Subota	*Soobota*
Sunday	Nedjelja	*Ned-yeh-lya*

English	Bosnian	Approx pronunciation
Morning	Jutro	*Yoo-tro*
Afternoon	Popodne	*Poh-pode-ne*
Night	Noć	*No-ch*
Yesterday	Juče	*Yoo-che*
Today	Danas	*Dahn-aas*
Tomorrow	Sutra	*Soo-tra*
What time is it?	Koliko je sati?	*Koh-lee-koh-yeh-saa-tee*
It is ...	Tačno ...	*Tah-ch-no*
Midday	Podne	*Pode-ne*
Midnight	Ponoć	*Poh-no-ch*

NUMBERS

English	Bosnian	Approx pronunciation
One	Jedan	*Yeh-dahn*
Two	Dva	*Dvah*
Three	Tri	*Tree*
Four	Četiri	*Chet-ee-ree*
Five	Pet	*Pate*
Six	Šest	*Shayst*
Seven	Sedam	*Seh-dahm*
Eight	Osam	*Oh-sum*
Nine	Devet	*Deh-vet*
Ten	Deset	*Deh-set*
Eleven	Jedanaest	*Yeh-dahn-ayst*
Twelve	Dvanaest	*Dvah-nay-st*
Twenty	Dvadeset	*Dvah-dehset*
Fifty	Pedeset	*Peh-dehset*
One hundred	Sto	*Stow*
One thousand	Hiljada	*Hill-ya-dah*

MONEY

English	Bosnian	Approx pronunciation
I would like to change these traveller's cheques/this money	Volio bi mjenjati ove čekove	*Voh-lee-oh bee me-yen-yaht-tee oh-veh check-oh-veh*
Where is an ATM?	Gdje je bankomat?	*g-dyeah-yeh-bankomat*
Do you accept credit cards?	Prihvatate li kreditne kartice?	*Pree-faht-te lee kred-eet-neh kar-tee-tze*

SIGNS & NOTICES

English	Bosnian	Approx pronunciation
Airport	Aerodrom	*Air-o-drome*
Toilets	Toalet	*Towalet*
Train station	Željeznička stanica	*Zheleznitchka stanica*
Platform	Platforma	*Platforma*

Emergencies

Emergency telephone numbers
Bosnia and Herzegovina
Emergency: *124*
Police: *122*
Fire: *123*
Emergency roadside service: *1282/1288*
Emergency service (*Hitna pomoć*),
Kolodvorska 14, Sarajevo. Tel: (033)
619 454, 618 062. Fax: (033) 655 939.
Email: hitnabih@bih.net.ba.
www.zhmpsarajevo.com
Sarajevo Pharmacy, Saliha
Hadžihuseinovića Muvekita 11,
Sarajevo. Tel: (033) 722 666. Fax: (033)
722 667. Email: apoteke@bih.net.ba.
www.apoteke-sarajevo.ba
Klinička bolnica Mostar (Medical
Clinic Mostar), *Kardinala A Stepenice*
bb, Mostar. Tel: (036) 313 238, 314 136,
322 712. Fax: (036) 327 750.

Serbia and Montenegro
Emergency medical aid: *94*
Fire: *93*
Police: *92*
Telephone information: *988*
Medical Urgent Centre, *Pasterova 2,*
Belgrade. Tel: (011) 3618 444, 3617 777.
www.klinicki-centar.co.yu

Health care
Montenegro and Serbia have
insurance agreements with over
20 countries. If you are eligible, this
means that you are not required to pay
for medical services in the case of an

emergency. It is best to check with
your health insurance agent before
taking a trip. Bosnia and Herzegovina
has no such agreements, and often
payment is expected at the time of
service. There are many private
practice clinics that offer good-quality
medical care.

Crime and scams
Look out for pickpockets in busy
places or in tramways and trains. Car
theft does happen, but violent crimes
are rare, especially against foreigners.
Women should always be cautious if
travelling alone, and avoid late-night
taxi rides. Walking in most old and
central parts of any city in the region
is quite safe.

EMBASSIES
Bosnia and Herzegovina
In case of emergency, it is
recommended that you contact your
embassy or consulate.
Australia
Mattiellistrasse 2–4, Vienna, Austria.
Tel: + 43 1 506 740. Fax: + 43 1 513
1656. Email: austemb@aon.at
Australian Honorary Consulate
Obala Kulina Bana 15/1, Sarajevo,
Bosnia and Herzegovina. Tel: (033) 251
230. Fax: (033) 251 238.
Canada
4 Grbavička, Sarajevo, Bosnia and
Herzegovina. Tel: (033) 222 033.

Fax: (033) 222 038.
Email: sjevo@dfait-maeci-gc.ca

Ireland
This embassy works through the UK Embassy in Sarajevo (*see below*).

New Zealand Consulate
Vlaska ulica 50a, Zagreb, Croatia. Tel/Fax: +385 1 615 1382. Email: nzealandconsulate@matis

South Africa
Budapest, Hungary (responsible for Croatia and Bosnia and Herzegovina). *Tel: +36 061 392 0999.*

UK
Tina Ujevića 8, Sarajevo, Bosnia and Herzegovina. Tel: (033) 282 200. Fax: (033) 282 203.
www.britishembassy.gov.uk.
Open: Mon–Thur 8.30am–5pm, Fri 8.30am–2.30pm.

USA
Alipašina 43, Sarajevo, Bosnia and Herzegovina. Tel: (033) 445 700. Fax: (033) 659 722.
www.sarajevo.usembassy.gov.
Open: Tue & Thur 8am–11.30, Mon, Wed, Fri 2–3.30pm, and by appointment.

Serbia

All information is available at *www.mfa.gov.yu*

Australia
Čika Ljubina 13, Belgrade. Tel: (011) 624 655. Fax: (011) 628 189, 3281 941 (imigraciono-visa section). Email: austemba@eunet.yu.
www.serbia.embassy.gov.au

Canada
Kneza Miloša 75, Belgrade. Tel: (011) 3063 000/039 (visa section). Fax: (011) 3063 042. Email: bgrad@dfait-maeci.gc.ca. www.canada.org.yu

UK
Resavska 46, Belgrade. Tel: (011) 645 055, 3061 070 (consular section). Fax: (011) 659 651. Email: ukembbg@eunet.yu.
www.britishembassy.gov.uk

USA
Kneza Miloša 50, Belgrade. Tel: (011) 3619 344. Fax: (011) 3615 489.
www.belgrade.usembassy.gov

Montenegro

UK
Bulevar Sv Petra Cetinjskog II/3, Podgorica. Tel: (081) 205 440. Fax: (081) 205 460. Email: britishoffice@cg.yu

USA
Kruševac bb, Podgorica. Tel: (081) 241 050, 241 052. Fax: (081) 241 371. Email: hyee@usaid.gov

For all other information, contact the Ministry of Foreign Affairs of the Republic of Serbia (*Kneza Miloša 24–26, Belgrade. Tel: (011) 3616 333*) or the Ministry of Foreign Affairs of the Republic of Montenegro (*Stanka Dragojevića 2, Podgorica, Montenegro. Tel: (081) 241 334*).

Directory

Accommodation price guide

The accommodation prices are based on the cost per person for two people sharing the least expensive double room with en suite bathroom and including breakfast.

★   Under €40
★★   €40–€75
★★★ Above €75

Eating out price guide

Price ranges are per person for a three-course meal without drinks.

★   €7–€12
★★   €12–€18
★★★ Above €18

BOSNIA AND HERZEGOVINA

Bjelašnica ski centre

ACCOMMODATION

Hotel Maršal ★★
This hotel is at the base of the ski lifts and has rooms for about 70 guests. It is a bargain if you are accustomed to the outrageous prices at ski resorts in the West. The ski lifts are three minutes away.
Babin Dol. Tel: (033) 279 100. Fax: (033) 279 149. Email: marshal@tksa.com.ba. www.hotel-marsal.ba

SPORT AND LEISURE

Ski Centar Bjelašnica
Branilaca Sarajeva 21. Tel: (033) 663 359. Fax: (033) 663 358. Email: info@bjelasnica.info

Blagaj

ACCOMMODATION

Hotel Ada ★★
Ada is the only hotel in Blagaj. The rooms are nice and have televisions and air conditioning. Each room has a balcony; ask for one facing the beautiful Buna River.
Branilaca Bosne bb. Tel: (036) 572 500/777. Fax: (036) 572 550. Email: motelada@bih.net.ba

Vila Ivanković ★★
A great place to stay to beat the summer heat, and only a short distance from Mostar. The rooms are excellent, with satellite televisions, mini-bars and air conditioning. The terrace bar and restaurant are also top quality and a favourite spot for locals.
Buna bb. Tel: (036) 480 830. Fax: (036) 480 831. Email: info@vila-ivankovic.com. www.vila-ivankovic.com

Foča

SPORT AND LEISURE

Encijan Rafting
Foča. Tel/Fax: (058) 211 150, (065) 626 588, 475 201, (069) 673 655. Email: encijan@teol.net, encijan@zona.ba. www.pkencijan.com

Jahorina ski centre

ACCOMMODATION

Hotel Kristal ★
The rooms are excellent

with good food to match. Rooms have satellite televisions, mini-bars and bath. The hotel also has a bar, restaurant, sauna and ski rental (and service). It is wise to make reservations a few months ahead of time.

Jahorina bb. Tel: (057) 226 574/725.

Hotel Nebojša ★
One of Jahorina's new hotels. This hotel sleeps 80 and has a great location near the top of the mountain just above Hotel Košuta. The rooms are good, and the hotel has a large 'ski garden' where many skiers gather to have a coffee or lunch.
Jahorina bb. Tel: (057) 270 500. Fax: (057) 270 500. Email: info@hotel-nebojsa.com. www.hotel-nebojsa.com

Hotel Termag ★★★
This new hotel is the best on the mountain. The architecture, interior, restaurant and rooms are decorated in the finest fashion. It's located near the lower ski lifts on Jahorina.
Poljice bb. Tel: (057) 272 100, 270 422. Email:

office@termaghotel.com. www.termaghotel.com

SPORT AND LEISURE
Ski Centar Jahorina
Jahorina bb. Tel: (065) 414 413. Email: info@jahorina.org

Konjic
SPORT AND LEISURE
Europe Rafting
One of two rafting agencies that have international certification on the Neretva River.
Kolonija 16, Konjic. Tel: (061) 817 209. Email: info@raftingeurope.com. www.raftingeurope.com

Salihamidžić Rafting
A small outfit with good boats and skippers who are internationally certified. The operator has a very reasonable place in Dejčići where you can enjoy excellent food after a long day on the river.
Dejčići bb, Konjic. Tel: (036) 724 175.

Mostar
ACCOMMODATION
PANSION ROSE ★
A great, inexpensive place just off the main boulevard in Donja Mahala. Comfy and clean

rooms with bathrooms, showers and televisions.
Bulevar bb. Tel/Fax: (036) 578 300. Email: info@pansion-rose.ba. www.pansion-rose.ba

Aparthotel Amicus ★★
This is a brand-new establishment with a swimming pool (making it nice in Mostar's summer heat). It is, however, a driving distance to the old town – or quite a long walk.
Put Hud br.3, Magistralni put M-17. Situated by the highway M17 on the northern entrance to Mostar (2km/1¼ miles from the old town), on the crossroads of Dubrovnik–Mostar–Sarajevo. Tel: (036) 501 900. Fax: (036) 501 930. Email: info@aparthotel-amicus.com. www.aparthotel-amicus.com

Kriva Ćuprija ★★
A new *pansion* just next to the Kriva Ćuprija in the old town. It's a great deal for the money and the location is second to none. The rooms and services are basic but new and quite agreeable:
Kriva Ćuprija 2. Tel: (061) 135 286.

Pansion Boticelli ★★

Family-owned B&B on the Radobolja River not far from the old bridge in the old town. It's a brand-new place with lovely terraces and décor. Certainly among the best places to stay in Mostar. *Muje Bjelavca 6. Tel: (063) 319 057.*

Pansion Most ★★

This private house is conveniently in Cernica, not far from the old bridge. *Adema Buče 100. Tel: (036) 552 528. Fax: (036) 552 660. Email: pansion_most@yahoo.com. www.pansionmostdzaba. com*

Bevanda ★★★

The rooms are large with chic art décor. Suites come with a large jacuzzi. *Stara Ilička bb. Tel: (036) 332 332. Fax: (036) 332 335. Email: hotel.bevanda@tel.net.ba. www.hotelbevanda.com*

EATING OUT

Babilon ★

This multi-terraced restaurant has one of the best views of the old bridge and the powerful Neretva River racing below it. The food is good and the servings are large. *Tabahana bb. Tel: (061) 164 912. Open: 9am–11pm. No credit cards.*

Oscar ★

A great outdoor place along the Radobolja River in the old town. One of the most comfy places to be found, with great food and drinks to match the atmosphere. *Ratanjska bb. Tel: (030) 793 555. Fax: (030) 792 550.*

Radobolja ★

Located at the source of the Radobolja River, this is a wonderfully refreshing spot for trout, Dalmatian specialities and good-quality *pršut* or ham. *Kraljice Katarine 11a. Tel: (036) 561 100, (061) 198 058. Fax: (036) 561 100. Open: 7am–midnight.*

Rondo ★

Known as one of the best restaurants in Mostar, this specialises in local and Dalmatian dishes and has a very comprehensive menu, excellent service and great prices. *Trg Hrvatskih Velikana bb. Tel: (036) 322 100. Open: 7am–midnight.*

Taurus ★

Traditional restaurant near the Kriva Ćuprija. It serves large portions of local, Italian and Dalmatian dishes. The rustic décor and fireplace make it a great place for dinner, and the small terrace on the Radobolja River is a great place for lunch. *Kriva Ćuprija 1. Tel: (061) 212 617. Open: 11am–midnight.*

Hindin Han ★★

You can't go wrong at this authentic traditional restaurant. Han specialises in locally made cheeses, meats and wines. *Jusovina bb. Tel: (036) 385 855, (061) 581 054. Email: hindin-han@mostar-tourist.info*

ENTERTAINMENT

Mo-Club

Housed in what used to be Tito's villa, this is one of Mostar's finest restaurants and a popular evening gathering place. *Mostarskogbataljona. Just across the river from Hotel Bristol. Tel: (036) 551 620. Open: 9am–midnight.*

Mount Velež

ACCOMMODATION

Motel Sunce ★

A wonderful, family-owned eco lodge on the Podveležje plateau. Simple rooms, fantastic food, great service and beautiful nature all around.

Email: info@motel-sunce-podvelez.com. www.motel-sunce-podvelez.com

Sarajevo

ACCOMMODATION

B&B Baščaršija ★

Certainly one of the nicest family-owned B&B in the city. The service is super friendly and the rooms quite nice and very clean.

Veliki Ćurčiluk 41. Tel: (033) 232 185; mobile: 061 177 952. Email: heartofthebascarsija@hotmail.com. Tram: 1, 2, 3, 5.

Campsite Oaza ★

This site is in Ilidža, about 30 minutes from the city centre. It has a full range of facilities for camping, including for camper vans, tents and basic bungalow accommodation.

Četvrte Viteške Brigade, Ilidža. Tel: (033) 636 142. Fax: (033) 636 140. Email:

info@hoteliilidza.ba. www.hoteliilidza.ba. Tram: 2, 3, 5, direction Baščaršija–Ilidža.

Ljubičica Hostel ★

This is the city's largest hostel. Most of the accommodation is located in private flats. The hostel offers a wide range of services including internet, safety deposit box, laundry and daily tours around and out of town.

Mula Mustafe Bašeskije 65. Tel: (033) 535 829. Email: taljubic@bih.net.ba. www.hostelljubicica.net. Tram: 1, 2, 3, 5.

Ada ★★

A new hotel situated right in the centre of the old town. This former embassy residence has been converted to a lovely small hotel with beautiful décor and good service.

Abdeshana 8. Tel: (033) 475 870, 537 145. Email: adahotel@adahotel.ba. www.adahotel.ba. Tram: 1, 2, 3, 5.

Hecco ★★

Located just a little up the north side of Baščaršija, this hotel is good value. Excellent service, great rooms, internet in each

room, and only a ten-minute walk to the old town.

Medrese 1. Tel: (033) 273 730. Fax: (033) 273 731. Email: info@hotel-hecco.net. www.hotel-hecco.net. Tram: 1, 2, 3, 5.

Hotel Terme ★★

This renovated thermal spa hotel has excellent and affordable accommodation as well as a full range of spa facilities – including jacuzzi, indoor heated pools and massage therapy. It is very near the Vrelo Bosne Park in Ilidža.

Hrasnička Cesta 14, Ilidža. Tel: (033) 772 000. Fax: (033) 772 001. Email: info@hoteliilidza.ba. www.hoteliilidza.ba. Tram: direction Baščaršija–Ilidža.

Hotel Villa Orient ★★

This hotel is in a superb location in the heart of the old town. Conveniently situated on a quiet side street near Sebilj Fountain, it's a bargain for a medium-price hotel.

Oprkanj 6. Tel: (033) 232 702. Fax: (033) 441 044.

Email: orient@bih.net.ba.
www.hotel-villa-
orient.com. Tram: 1, 2, 3, 5.

Astra ★★★

This hotel is at the upper end of Sarajevo's central hotels. The rooms and facilities are very good but the rooms are not very spacious.
Zelenih Beretki 9. Tel: (033) 252 100/200. Fax: (033) 209 939. Email: h.astravbih.net.ba. www.hotel-astra.com.ba. Tram: 1, 2, 3, 5.

EATING OUT

Bosna ★

One of the classic *pita* places in the old town. It's always crowded and for a reason. The *pita* (filo-dough pastry dish made with cheese, spinach or potato) is baked fresh all day and the service is quick and friendly.
Bravadžiluk 11. Tel: (033) 538 426. Open: 8am–10pm.

Global Foods ★

It's worth an inexpensive taxi from the city centre to this family-owned and run restaurant. One of the few places to serve falafel, hummus and other Middle Eastern dishes as well as organic and domestic wines.
Braće Begića 6. Tel: (061) 274 955. Open: Mon–Sat 11am–11pm. Closed: Sun. No credit/debit cards.

Kod Bibana ★

A must-do in Sarajevo. It's best to take a taxi because the restaurant is quite far up the hill on the southern slopes of the old town. The views are magnificent and the food is wholesome and tasty. It's a laidback place and a favourite spot for locals, young and old.
Hošin Brijeg 95. Tel: (033) 232 026. Open: 10am–10pm. No credit/debit cards.

Metropolis ★

Quite possibly the best place in town for its prices, choice, quality and location. It's a local favourite for lunches, snacks, coffee breaks and great cakes and ice cream. It also has a great breakfast menu which is hard to come by in Sarajevo.
Maršala Tita 21. Tel: (033) 203 315. Open: Mon–Fri 8am–11pm, Sat 9am–11pm, Sun 11am–11pm.

Pod Lipom ★

Some of the best traditional food in the old town. Pod Lipom has been around for ages and is a favourite spot for locals. If may be difficult to find a table, but it's worth waiting or coming back later to try your luck. It's definitely one of the best deals in town.
Prote Bakovića 8 i 6. Tel: (033) 440 700. Open: 8am–midnight. No credit/debit cards.

Ramis ★

This is the legendary sweet shop of Sarajevo. Ramis is just on the artificial border, where the old Turkish quarter ends and the Austro-Hungarian begins. Cake and coffee are very inexpensive and the cakes are made fresh daily.
Sarači 1. Tel: (033) 535 947. Open: 9am–10pm.

Sač ★

This is one of the few places in the old town where they make *pita* the old way, in the 'Dutch oven' (*ispod sača*), baked with coals in a large metal pan. Every sort of *pita* is delicious and you can see how it is made.

Mali Bravadžiluk 2. Tel: (061) 439 045. Open: 8am–11pm.

Željo ★

It is said that you haven't visited Sarajevo if you haven't eaten *ćevapi* (small meat sausages) at Željo. Željo is named after the local football club and it is dead serious about its *ćevapi*. It is so popular that they opened up another shop next door to the original one!

Kundurdžiluk 1. Tel: (033) 447 000. Open: 8am–10pm.

Hacienda Cantina Mexicana ★★

There are only a few Mexican restaurants in and Hacienda is the only one in the old town. The portion sizes are very generous and the cocktails are popular with foreign guests. The restaurant is upstairs while downstairs is one of the best bars in town.

Bazerdžani 3. Tel: (033) 441 918. www. haciendasarajevo.com. Open: Mon–Fri 10am–11pm, Sat & Sun 10am–1am. No credit/debit cards.

Jež ★★

This restaurant is in an old Austro-Hungarian building near the National Gallery. The food, service and atmosphere are great, and the prices are extremely reasonable. The menu has a wide array of international dishes.

Zelenih Beretki 14. Tel: (033) 650 312. Open: Mon–Sat 9am–11pm, Sun 5pm–11pm.

Karuso ★★

Sarajevo's only 'vegetarian' restaurant (they also serve fresh fish and sushi). This tiny restaurant has fantastic food and is a no-smoking establishment. The menu consists of daily specials that the cook, Sasha, designs himself. The fish is fresh as are all the ingredients that Sasha uses.

Dženetića Čikma. Tel: (033) 444 647. Open: Mon–Sat noon–3pm, 6pm–11pm. Closed: Sun.

Mala Kuhinja ★★

This is a new restaurant that caters to whatever you fancy. The chef will personally wait on you and prepare what you would like with the daily ingredients available. It's a tiny place, but it's well worth making sure you eat at least one meal here.

Josipa Stadlera 8. Tel: (061) 144 741. Open: Mon–Fri 9am–6pm, Sat 9am–7pm. Closed: Sun.

Park Prinčeva ★★

Try to arrive before sunset when dining at Park Prinčeva. This restaurant boasts the best view in town and certainly has the food and atmosphere to match. It often has soft live traditional music, which goes perfectly with the traditional menu.

Iza Hrida 7. Tel: (061) 222 708. Fax: (033) 532 403. www.parkprinceva.ba. Open: 9am–11.30pm.

To Be ★★

This tiny restaurant is on one of the many side streets in the old town. The food is top grade, and so is the service. To Be has a very cosy and intimate atmosphere and is perfect for couples. The steak is fantastic, as are the vegetarian soup and vegetarian platter.

Čizmedžiluk 5. Tel: (033) 233 265. Open: noon–11pm. No credit/debit cards.

ENTERTAINMENT

City Pub

A spacious and lively bar on the street running parallel to Ferhadija walkway, towards the river. City Pub could quite possibly be the best bar in town with great drink prices, a friendly atmosphere, and frequent live music and DJs.

Hadžiristića bb. Tel: (033) 209 789. Open: 10am–2am.

Halvat (Tea shop)

No food here, but the best-kept secret in the heart of the old town. The tea shop is similar to the *shisha* (water pipe) places found in Istanbul. It serves Turkish, Moroccan and other tea as well as Bosnian coffee. The *shishas* are packed with apple- or honey-flavoured tobacco and this is a great place to chill out Oriental style.

Luledžina 6. Tel: (061) 515 713. Open: 9am–11pm.

Kamerni Teatar 55 (Chamber Theatre 55)

This is hands down the best place to see local theatre productions. Many of Sarajevo's best actors and actresses are members of this small but very active theatre house. It is on Titova Street near the Vječna Vatra (Eternal Flame).

Maršala Tita 56/II. Tel: (033) 471 184. Fax: (033) 471 184. Email: kamerni@Isinter.net. Tickets are sold at the venue.

Karabit (Café)

This café has the city's finest selection of organic and exotic teas, freshly squeezed juices, local wines, spirits and beer.

Zelenih Beretki 8. Located on the bottom floor of the National Gallery. Tel: (033) 712 010. Fax: (033) 712 011. Email: vedad.d@buybook.ba. www.buybook.ba

Kino Obala (Cinema)

On the south bank of the Miljacka River, this is the most modern and comfortable cinema in the city, often with English subtitles.

Hamdije Kreševljakovića 13. Tel: (033) 668 186/187.

Mash (Bar)

This remains one of the best bars in the city. Just next to the National Theatre, every evening it is packed with a hip and laidback crowd. There is a live DJ and the bar serves excellent food to complement the great atmosphere.

Branilaca Sarajeva 20/1. Tel: (062) 295 369. Open: Mon–Fri 8.30am–1am, Sat & Sun 9am–3am.

Pivnica (Bar)

Sarajevo's legendary brewery now has a large bar and restaurant. It serves the only local draught dark beer in the country. The food and beer are excellent. Food is served late as well, and this is a popular destination for Sarajevo's thirty somethings.

Franjevačka 15. Tel: (033) 239 740. Open: 10am–1am.

SPORT AND LEISURE

Ciklo Centar (Cycling)

Ilidža is an ideal place for a walk or a jog down the Aleja, which is a 2km ($1^1/_4$-mile) walking and jogging area around the Vrelo Bosne Park. Near the park, this outfit rents bicycles for the day. It also organises mountain-biking trips in the mountains.

Hamze Čelenke 58, Ilidža.

Tel: (033) 625 243. Email:
bikeshop@bih.net.ba.
www.ciklocentar.com
Green Visions (Hiking
and walking)
A Sarajevo-based eco-
tourism group organising
daily hikes around Bosnia
and Herzegovina from
April to October.
The group provides
transport, guides and
lunch.
Radnička bb. Tel: (033)
717 290, 061 213 278.
Email:
sarajevo@greenvisions.ba.
www.greenvisions.ba
Terme Ilidža (Swimming)
In the suburb of Ilidža,
there is a brand-new
indoor/outdoor swimming
pool complex. There is
also a café and small
restaurant there, making it
an ideal place to spend
the entire day.
Mala Aleja 40 (behind
Dom Zdravlje). Tel: (033)
771 011. Fax: (033) 771
010. Email: info@terme-
ilidza.ba. www.terme-
ilidza.ba. Swimming pool
open: 9am–9pm.
Admission charge.
Tropical garden open:
8am–10pm. Restaurant
open: 8.30am–10.30pm.
Tramways from the city

centre to the last station in
Ilidža run all day long.
From the last tram stop, it
is a mere 5-minute walk.

Sutjeska National Park
ACCOMMODATION
Mladosť Hotel ★
This is the only
accommodation in the
park with facilities.
A socialist-era hotel with
simple rooms and not-so-
inspiring décor.
Tjentište bb. Tel: (058) 520
107/114. Email:
sutjeska@teol.net.
www.sutjeska.net

Travnik
ACCOMMODATION
Aba ★
This is a small *pansion*
near Plava Voda. There
are very pleasant
apartments equipped
with a new jacuzzi and
modern furniture.
Šumeće 166a. Tel: (030)
511 462.
Bajra ★
This is an excellent new
motel near the centre of
town. The rooms are
modern and quite nice.
The restaurant is excellent
as is the service.
Dolac na Lašvi bb.
Tel: (030) 516 110.

Pansion-restoran Oniks ★
This B&B is in the old
quarter of Travnik, not far
from the Šarena Džamija
(Multi-coloured Mosque).
The rooms are small but
pleasant and the
restaurant serves
traditional food.
Donja Čaršija-Žitarnica
bb. Tel: (030) 512 182.

EATING OUT
Kuća Ive Andrića ★
A relaxed but somewhat
classy place with a great
summer garden. It serves
traditional meals, many of
which are made in the
ispod saća (Dutch
oven). It is very
reasonably priced and a
great place to have a
meal after visiting the
museum upstairs.
Mehmed-Paše Kukavice 1.
Tel: (030) 518 140, 541 590.
Plava Voda ★
This restaurant is
something of a historical
monument and the rule is
that anybody visiting
Travnik should visit Plava
Voda, both for the lovely
water and for the food.
Don't miss this one.
Šumeće 14. Tel: (030) 512
171, (061) 798 040. Open:
7am–11pm.

Restoran Lutvina Kahva ★

This cosy place is on the crystal-clear waters of Plava Voda. It serves traditional meals on the summer terrace that are delicious. The service is good and the food is very reasonably priced.

Plava Voda bb, Šumeće. Tel: (061) 154 520. Open: 7am–11pm.

Trebinje
ACCOMMODATION
Hotel Leotar ★★

On the southeast side of the river, this is the main hotel from the Yugoslavia days.

Tel: (059) 261 082.

Platani Hotel ★★

Small with pleasant rooms, a restaurant and café.

Cvjetni Trg1. Tel: (059) 225 134/135.

Uzice
SPORT AND LEISURE
Tourist Office of Užice (Mountain biking)

Tel: (031) 513 485. Email: office@turizamuzica.org.yu

Visoko
ACCOMMODATION
Motel Bosnian Pyramid of the Sun ★★

Located in the centre of Visoko, this motel is brand new, and the rooms are comfortable.

Musala 1. Tel/Fax: (032) 731 460/461, (061) 587 926. Email: info@motelpiramidasunca. co.ba. www.motelpiramidasunca. co.ba

EATING OUT
Ćevabdžinica Ihtijarević ★

These *Ćevabdžinicas* are famous small grills that cook excellent and inexpensive meals.

Čaršijska 40. Tel: (032) 737 136. Open: 7am–11pm.

No.1 ★

This restaurant offers a taste of traditional Bosnian food and pizzas with a choice of alcoholic or non-alcoholic drinks.

Mule Hodžića 108. Tel: (032) 735 195. Open: 9am–11pm.

SERBIA
Belgrade
ACCOMMODATION
Belgrade Eye Hostel ★

A former family house turned into a hostel that offers a surprising level of comfort at very reasonable rates. Private rooms with bathroom are available as well as dorms.

Krunska 6b. Tel: (064) 2588 754. Email: belgradeeye@gmail.com

Hostel Tis ★

Once a large house, this has now been converted into a hostel. It has a spacious garden and a large living room. Tis is in the Vračar neighbourhood in the old part of town; it's a perfect hostel location right in the middle of Belgrade's nightlife districts and good restaurants. It is a ten-minute bus or tram ride to the city centre. The rooms are clean and safe.

Koste Abraševića 17. Tel: (011) 3806 050. Email: terranova@sbb.co.yu

Hotel Royal ★★

Fantastic mid-range hotel in the centre of town. Good value for the price, and close to shopping streets, the Kalemegdan Fortress and the best nightlife spots.

Kraja Petra 56. Tel: (011) 2634 222. Fax: (011) 2626 459. Email: toplice@net.yu

Hotel Le Petit Piaf ★★★

A wonderful location in the centre of Belgrade in Skadarlija. Dozens of

restaurants and cafés are at your doorstep in the Belgrade bohemian quarter. The rooms are basic but offer a good range of services.
Skadarska 34. Tel: (011) 3035 858/353. Email: office@petitpiaf.com. www.petitpiaf.com

Hotel Moskva ★★★
One of Belgrade's finest hotels. Constructed in 1906 and fully renovated in 1973, this Belgrade classic couldn't be more central. It is located just off the Knez Mihailova, Belgrade's main pedestrian street, home to the main shopping areas, art galleries and the National Theatre. At the end of the street is the Kalemegdan Park. The hotel's rooms are spacious with all modern facilities. The service is excellent and the café bar is a popular spot in town.
Balkanska1. Tel: (011) 2686 255. Fax: (011) 2688 389. Email: hotelmoskva@absolutok.net. www.hotelmoskva.co.yu

EATING OUT
Restaurant '?' ★
Across from Saborna church, this is the oldest restaurant in Belgrade and was built in 1823. The restaurant has maintained its original style, and the traditional sausages and the hot *rakija* (plum brandy) are house specialities.
Kralja Petra 1 br.6. Tel: (011) 635 421. Open: 7am–11pm.

Tri Šešira ★
An affordable restaurant with tasty food in the old bohemian quarter of Skadarlija.
Skadarska 29. Tel: (011) 324 7501. Open: 11am–1am.

Dačo ★★
The restaurant specialises in traditional Serbian food. It has created a rural Serbian ambience and the waiting staff wear traditional attire. All of the dishes are house specialities.
Patrisa Lumumbe 49. Tel: (011) 2781 009. Open: Tue–Sun noon–midnight. Closed: Mon.

Dišina Koliba ★★
The owners of this restaurant have created a warm and hospitable atmosphere with pleasant background music. The cuisine is generally traditional with excellent lamb and pork dishes. Try the exceptional cheeses and young *kajmak* (cream cheese spread).
2v Andre Nikolića. Tel: (011) 369 1700. Open: Mon–Sat 11am–11pm, Sun noon–8pm.

Šešir Moj ★★
Alongside its traditional cuisine, this classic Skadarlija bohemian restaurant organises literary evenings and various cultural manifestations. The wine selection is also good, and this is a great place for late-night dining and drinking.
Skadarska 21. Tel: (011) 322 8750. Open: 9am–1am.

ENTERTAINMENT
Andergraund (Nightclub)
The concept of this club is generally focused on electronic music. It's a balanced mix of alternative and mainstream, and there are frequent live concerts.
Pariska 1a. Tel: (011) 2625 681, (063) 407 070. www.andergraund.com. Open: 10am–8pm & 10pm–6am.

Bitef Art Café (Nightclub)
This club has a cultish clientele with various art shows, great lights and music. It has chic décor and is quite popular in the daytime as well as in the evening.
Skver Mire Trailović 1. Tel: (063) 594 294.

Bitef Teatar (Theatre)
Skver Mire Trailović 1. Tel: (011) 3243 108/109, 3245 241. Fax: (011) 3243 966. Email: production@bitef.co.yu

Café Club 'No Limit'
The name says it all. Serves as a café during the day and a bar in the evening.
Bulevar Despota Stefana 67. Email: YUnolimit@ hotmail.com. www. nolimit.scriptmania.com

Dom Sindikata (Cinema)
Trg Nikole Pašića 5. Tel: (011) 3234 849.

Jugoslovensko Dramsko Pozorište (Yugoslav Drama Theatre)
Kralja Milana 50. Tel: (011) 644 447, 3061 900/906. www.jdp.co.yu

Pozorište Atelje 212 (Theatre Atelje 212)
Svetogorska 21. Tel: (011) 3246 146/147/148. Fax:

(011) 3236 215. Email: atelje@hotmail.com

Roda Intermezzo Cineplex (Cinema)
Požeška 83a. Tel: (011) 2545 260.

Srpska Kafana (Serbian Tavern)
One of the favourite bohemian bars in the city. Established in 1936, this tavern has served its fair share of beers. Many of Belgrade's arts crowd frequents here. The tavern also serves traditional local food.
Svetogorska 25. Tel: (011) 3247 197. Open: 10am–midnight.

Tuckwood Cineplex (Cinema)
Kneza Miloša 7. Tel: (011) 3236 517.

Kopaonik

ACCOMMODATION

Hotel Putnik ★★
Hotel Putnik is only 200m (219yds) from the ski lifts. This is a pre-war hotel that is in good shape, and it offers comfortable two- and three-bed rooms. It also has small shops and a large terrace café overlooking the mountain.
Tel: (036) 71 030, 71 038. Fax: (036) 71 069.

Hotel Grand ★★★
This modern and comfortable hotel is situated in the central part of Genex Tourist Centre, near the first ski lifts, with beautiful panoramic views of the forest-covered slopes of Kopaonik. It offers the best accommodation and service on the mountain as well as a full range of tourism services, including skiing, hiking and biking.
Tel: (036) 71 027. Email: hgrand@icg.co.yu

SPORT AND LEISURE

Travel Agency Genex-Kopaonik (Skiing)
Tel: (036) 71 049.

Novi Sad

ACCOMMODATION

Boarding House Saint George ★
Close to the Danube River and the Petrovaradin Fortress, this family-owned and run B&B has friendly staff and a homely feel. The rooms are excellent with lovely décor, and the staff speak fluent English.
Marina Držića, Petrovaradin.

Tel/Fax: (021) 432 332.
Email: mailto:info@
svetigeorgije.co.yu
Fontana ★
One of the better places
in town for the price. The
rooms are stylish with new
facilities, and there is also
a large apartment.
Fontana has friendly and
helpful staff.
Nikole Pašića 17. Tel: (021)
6621 779.
Hotel Boem ★
A great place to stay, just
a little out of town near
Fruška Gora National
Park. The hotel is basic
but rather nice, and it
is in the general vicinity
of monasteries and
vineyards.
Branka Radičevića 5,
Sremski Karlovci
(7km/4¹/₃ miles from Novi
Sad). Tel: (021) 881
038/892. Email:
hoem@eunet.yu
Hotel Zenit ★★
The best location for
being in the centre of it
all. Zenit has full-service
rooms and modern
facilities. It is in walking
distance from most
attractions in Novi Sad.
Zmaj Jovina 8.
Tel: (021) 621 444/035.
Fax: (021) 6621 327.

EATING OUT
Chinese Fast Food ★
Fruškogorska 18. Tel: (021)
6350 543.
Fontana ★
A great budget place with
good soups, Bosnian
ćevapi (small meat
sausages) and grilled
mixed meat. The staff are
friendly and the terrace is
a great spot for lunch.
Nikole Pašića 17.
Tel: (021) 6621 779.
Open: 9am–11pm.
Marina ★
A budget restaurant that
is a local favourite known
for its great food. Just a
few minutes away from
the city centre.
Trg Mladenaca 4. Tel: (021)
424 353. Open: 8am–11pm.
Does deliveries.
Salaš 84 ★
Everyone raves about
Salas 84. It's about a
30km (18¹/₂-mile) drive
towards Fruška Gora,
and attracts locals from
all over the region.
The food and service
are excellent.
Vojvodanskih Brigada
17/I. Tel: (021) 445 993,
(065) 5445 993.
Fax: (021) 6417 263.
www.salas84.co.yu.
Open: 9.30am–10pm.

Surabaja ★
If you're looking for a
change from traditional
food and lots of meat, this
Indonesian restaurant is a
good alternative.
Primorska 26. Tel: (021)
6413 400.
Plava Frajla ★★
This is a traditional cuisine
establishment. The food is
extremely fresh; they even
bake their own bread. The
desserts are fantastic, and
over the weekends there is
live music.
Sutjeska 2. Tel: (021) 6613
675, 4882 420. Email:
info@plavafrajla.co.yu.
www.plavafrajla.co.yu.
Open: Mon–Thur & Sun
9am–midnight, Fri & Sat
9am–1am.
Pomodoro Rosso ★★
Located in the very centre
of the city, this serves
some of Novi Sad's best
Italian dishes. The owners
have created an authentic
Italian atmosphere,
inspired by the city of
Modena.
Nikole Pašića 14. Tel: (021)
424 023, (065) 4825 452.
Email:
info@pomodororosso.com.
www.pomodororosso.com.
Open: 9am–midnight.
Closed: Sun.

ENTERTAINMENT

Bioskop Arena (Cinema)
Bulevar Mihajla Pupina.
Tel: (021) 615 760.

**Bioskop Kulturnog
Centra Novog Sada –
KCNS (Novi Sad Cultural
Centre Cinema)**
*Katolička porta 5. Tel:
(021) 528 346. Email:
kcns@EUnet.yu*

Bistro (Bar)
Generally the bar is
dimmed but there is a
friendly atmosphere.
It serves a young,
alternative crowd, with
music and live DJs on
occasions.
Ulica Modene.

Lounge Café Club
A small café with great
music and a friendly
atmosphere. It is
dedicated to the music
scene and offers various
flavours of modern
tunes, including broken
beat, nujazz, soul,
funky, deep house and
chill music.
*Zmaj Jovina 10. Email:
office@loungecafe.info*

**Srpsko Narodno Pozorište
(Serbian National
Theatre)**
*Pozorišni Trg 1. Tel: (021)
520 091, 451 452.*

SPORT AND LEISURE

**Železničar Association of
Mountaineers and Skiers
(Hiking)**
This outfit organises a
hiking trip every Sunday
on Fruška Mountain and
in the Novi Sad vicinity.
*Trg Galerija 4. Tel: (021)
529 978. Email:
zeleznicar.nsad@neobee.net*

Vrnjačka Banja
ACCOMMODATION

Villa San ★
A classic early 20th-
century villa, San offers
eight very nice, spacious
and comfortable
apartments. It also has a
restaurant with both
traditional and
international cuisine, and
often hosts live music.
*Vrnjačka bb. Tel: (036) 612
150/564. Email:
htpfontana@ptt.yu*

Hotel Aleksandar ★★
Located in the centre of
Vrnjačka thermal spa,
very near the central park
and promenade. This
hotel offers the rare
services of organising
local excursions to some
of the region's tourist
sites. The hotel itself has
good service, and the
rooms, although nothing

fancy, are large and
comfortable.
*Čajkina 7. Tel: (036) 61
799. Email: office@
aleksandarhotel.com.
www.aleksandar-
hotel.co.yu*

Hotel Borjak ★★
The tourist settlement of
Borjak is in a large park
near to the source of the
mineral spring Snežnik.
*Bulevar Srpskih Vladara
bb. Tel: (036) 661 263.*

EATING OUT

Kraljica ★★
This Serbian restaurant is
in the centre of town at
the beginning of the main
promenade and city
market. They serve many
barbecue specialities and
'Dutch oven' (*ispod sača*)
breads and meats.
*Nemanjina 22. Tel: (036)
611 565, (063) 7773 540.
Open: 7.30am–midnight.*

Kruna ★★
This old-style restaurant is
next to three of the most
well-known thermal
springs: Snežnik, Jezera
and Slatine. For winter
visitors, there is a lovely
fireplace hall, and for
summer guests the
summer garden has a
cooling fountain and

overlooks the springs' lake. Every evening there is the old town acoustic orchestra for entertainment.
Slatinski Venac 3.
Tel: (036) 613 513.

Savka ★★
This restaurant has a large international menu with a surprising choice of cocktails. It is located in an old villa in the central part of town and frequently organises live music.
Gavrila Principa 6. Tel: (036) 617 434.

Zlatibor
ACCOMMODATION
Hotel Zlatibor ★★
A little on the 'old school' side, but offers basic, clean and reasonably priced accommodation. It is centrally situated near the lake, bus station and the area's tourist attractions.
Naselje Jezero 26.
Tel: (031) 841 021.
Fax: (031) 841 183.

Vila Milena ★★
The villa is largely constructed of natural materials, adding to its natural ambience. The rooms are basic but

have modern facilities. The villa is situated just behind the ski lift and near the shopping centre.
Tel: (031) 841 222, (064) 2782 525. Email: vilamilena@ptt

Vila Mirjana ★★
Mirjana paid close attention to the interior design of this lovely little villa tucked between a pine and birch tree forest. The rooms are cosy with lots of natural light, and the hotel has both a modern and family feel to it.
Tel: (064) 2300 188.
www.vilamirjana.co.yu

EATING OUT
Miris Dunja ★★
This establishment has a specific ambience, similar to that of an old village family home. It has a great variation of old rural specialities made from fresh dairy, meat and local produce. The restaurant is in the Obudovica settlement near the Palisad hotel.
Obudovica 32. Tel: (031) 841 529, (064) 322 40 55.
Open: 7pm–2am.

Park ★★
Located in Durkovac, Park is in a lovely natural environment. The establishment's owner is a professional cook with rich experience in both Mediterranean dishes and local cuisine. This is one of the few places where you can find true regional Zlatibor dishes.
Durkovac 51. Tel: (031) 841 818. Open: 9am–11pm.

SPORT AND LEISURE
Tourist Office Zlatibor (Mountain biking)
Jezero bb, Čajetina.
Tel: (031) 841 646.
Fax: (031) 841 244.
Email: toz@ptt.yu.
www.zlatibor.co.yu
Turistička Agencija Miros (Excursions)
Tržni Centar. Tel/Fax: (031) 845 000, (063) 666 768.

MONTENEGRO
Bar
ACCOMMODATION
Sidro ★
This simple but cosy motel is near the town centre and the coast.
Obala 13. jula. Tel/Fax: (085) 312 425/200. Email: sidro@lukabar.cg.yu.
www.lukabar.cg.yu

Vila Aleksandar ★★
Situated near Sutomore beach, about 7km (4¹/₃ miles) from Bar. This peaceful villa is near the beach in a grove of olives and mandarins.
Tel: (085) 374 240, 370 024, 312 885. Fax: (085) 312 909, (067) 403 550. Email: stevo86@cg.yu.
www.vilaaleksandar.com

EATING OUT

Kod Džema ★
Mainly a seafood restaurant, it specialises in catches of the day, and fresh fish brought in daily from the Adriatic is served here. They have wonderful fish soup. Don't let the location put you off.
Željeznička Stanica.

Donna Kod Nikole ★★
Specialising in seafood and Mediterranean cuisine, this restaurant also serves the classical local meat dishes. The terrace is the best option on a summer's evening.
Gradska Marina. Tel: (086) 451 531, (069) 330 332.
Open: 9am–2am.

Garden Café ★★
This classic Italian restaurant near the old town serves both lunch and dinner. It has tasty salads for a light lunch and serves good local wines.
Mediteranska bb. Tel: (067) 351 155. Email: rvadjon@cg.yu.
www.budva.com. Open: 7.30am–1am.

Marina ★★
This restaurant is in, well yes, the marina. It serves good international food at extremely low rates.
Gat 5, Obala 13. jula. Tel: (085) 317 785.
Open: 10am–11pm.

Budva

ACCOMMODATION

Hotel Fontana ★★
A small, privately owned hotel in the centre of town. The room décor is simple but nice and there is good service.
Slovenska Obala 23.
Tel: (086) 452 153. Email: fontana@budva.com

Konoba Galeb ★★
Established in 1966, Galeb is one of the oldest private restaurants in Budva. It serves tasty shellfish and has a great shrimp scampi.
Vrzdak, Stari Grad.
Tel: (086) 456 546, (069) 651 881. Open: 11am–1am.

Lučić-Garni Hotel ★★
Centrally located in Budva very near the beach, bus station and supermarkets, this hotel is comfy and convenient for walking everywhere.
Jadranski Put 37.
Tel: (086) 403 900, 452 167.
Email: hotel_lucic@yahoo.com

Bella Vista ★★★
A modern hotel a short drive from Budva. It has excellent service and great rooms. Well worth the drive for the peace and tranquil atmosphere.
Bečići. Tel: (086) 453 975, 451 445. Email: bellavista@cg.yu.
www.bellavista.co.yu

Hotel Max Prestige ★★★
With 11 luxury rooms, all fully equipped and offering maximum comfort.
Žrtava Fašizma bb.
Tel: (086) 458 330, 403 068.
Fax: (086) 458 350.
Email: maxprestige@cg.yu.
www.hotelmaxprestige.com

Zamak Pobore ★★★
The Zamak complex's décor is styled like an old castle. This charming little hotel is in the foothills, with great views, easy access, and peace and quiet.

*Pobori bb. Tel: (086) 464
601/602. Fax: (086) 464
603. Email:
office@zamak.com*

EATING OUT
Picasso ★

A restaurant, café and
pizzeria. It's a popular
lunch spot and many
locals go just for the
good coffee.
*Trg Palmi, Stari Grad.
Tel: (086) 402 804.
Open: 8am–midnight.*

ENTERTAINMENT
Greco (Café bar)

A laidback café bar with
a lovely summer garden
covered in vines to keep
it cool.
*Njegoševa 17, Stari Grad.
Tel: (069) 040 332. Open:
9am–midnight.*

Maestral Casino

A casino in the Maestral
Resort.
*Maestral Resort &
Casino, Pržno. Tel: (086)
410 100. Open: Mon–Fri
6pm–4am, Sat & Sun
noon–5am.
www.maestral.info*

Ričardova Glava
(Café bar)

A very popular café and
bar on the beach. Many
locals flock to the

'Richard's Head', and
it's a convenient place
to take a break from
the beach and have
a cool drink.
*Mogren beach. Open:
11pm–5am.
www.trocaderoclub.com*

SPORT AND LEISURE
Deep 'n' Blue (Diving)

Diving lessons and
excursions plus other
activities like hiking and
sailing trips.
Tel: (069) 030 003.

Tennis Club Budva

*Dositejeva 26.
Tel: (086) 451 236.*

Tourist Agency 'Del Mar'
(Waterskiing)

This outfit can arrange
waterski rentals for the
Budva area.
*Tel/Fax: (069) 560 300,
(086) 452 476. Email:
delmar@cg.yu*

Cetinje
ACCOMMODATION
Ivanova Korita ★

For a nice nature stay, this
hotel (the name means
'Ivan's River Beds') has
simple accommodation, a
children's summer camp,
and a newly renovated
mountain lodge. It is
located at Ivan's River

Bed and near Njegoš'
mausoleum in Lovćen
National Park.
*Brajova 2. Tel: (086) 233
700, 230 530. Fax: (086)
233 700. Email:
odmaraliste@cg.yu*

Hotel Grand ★★

One of Montenegro's
oldest hotels, in the old
courthouse in the centre
of town. It largely caters
for sports tourism, but
regularly accommodates
tourists visiting Cetinje.
*Tel: (086) 242 400. Email:
hotelgrand@cg.yu*

Panorama Gazivoda ★★

On the road towards
Podgorica, this new hotel
has six rooms and two
apartments with modest
but adequate
accommodation. It has a
beautiful view of the
Crnojević River.
*Tel: (081) 712 037. Email:
hotel.gazivoda@chello.at*

EATING OUT
Belveder ★★

It's hard to judge which is
better, the view of the
Crnojević River and Lake
Skadar or the great
national cuisine. Located
on the way from
Podgorica towards
Cetinje, this large open-air

restaurant serves both local meat and fish dishes. The service is excellent and the fish is caught daily, either in the river or in the lake; the trout is first class.

Kruševo Ždrijelo.
Tel: (086) 235 282.
Email: belveder@cg.yu.
Open: 9am–midnight.

Konak ★★

This inexpensive restaurant not only serves traditional cuisine but does its best to prepare vegetarian food as well. It's a nice lunch spot, with traditional décor and a good selection of cheeses.

Zabrde bb. 4km
(2¹/₂ miles) from Cetinje
on the route to Budva.
Tel: (086) 761 011.
www.konak.cg.yu.
Open: 24 hours.

Posljednja Luka ★★

Translated, the restaurant's name means 'The Last Dock' – the owner worked for many years as a ship's cook before he hung up his sailing hat and opened his own restaurant. He makes his own wine and a few fish specialities that are hard to find. If you're a seafood lover, try the eel if you dare!

Potpočivalo, Rijeka
Crnojevića. Tel: (086) 239
527, (067) 539 119.
Open: noon–8pm.

Vidikovac ★★

Although the food is quite good, everyone comes here for the views. At one side is Lovćen Mountain and at the other the Adriatic. On a clear day you can easily see both. It's a perfect lunch spot when visiting Njegoš' mausoleum.

On the road towards
Njegoš' mausoleum.
Tel: (085) 458 178.

ENTERTAINMENT

Piper's Café and Bar

With large outdoor seating, this is a perfect place to beat the heat under the shade of the 100-year-old linden trees.

In the square between
Lovćenska Vila (Lovćen
Villa) and Vlaška Crkva
(Vlach Church).

Yellow Moon (Café)

A classic café that serves good coffee and has a nice outside shaded terrace in the heart of town.

Njegoševa Ulica. Open:
9am–2am.

Kolašin

SPORT AND LEISURE

Turistička Agencija (Eco-tours)

Based in the northern highlands of Montenegro, this experienced agency offers hiking and rafting in and around the national park.

Kolašin. Tel: (069) 028 831,
(081) 864 140.

Kotor

ACCOMMODATION

Spasic-Masera ★

A clean and simple youth hostel that is open during the summer months.

Dobrota. Tel: (082) 330
258/254. Email:
sdomkotor@cg.yu.
www.hostelkotor.com

Sind ★★

Situated in an adapted old school building, the interior is modern and the service quite good.

Muo bb. Tel: (082) 336 201.
Fax: (082) 301 400. Email:
sindcentar@cg.yu.
www.sindcentar.cg.yu

Vardar ★★

Ideally located in the centre of the old town, this hotel has a restaurant and bar. Rooms are basic but each has its own bath. Ask for the room with the terrace.

Stari Grad bb. Tel: (082) 325 084/086. Fax: (082) 325 074. Email: vardar@cg.yu

Splendido ★★★

Certainly one of the best places to stay in the Kotor area, this attractive and modern hotel is in the small village of Prčanj. Built at the base of the steep walls of Kotor Bay, the views are magnificent and the rooms and service are excellent.

Glavati bb, Prčanj. Tel: (082) 301 700. Fax: (082) 336 222. Email: hotel.splendido@cg.yu

EATING OUT

Elas ★★

A refreshing change to the similar menus throughout the region, Ellas serves good Greek food prepared in the traditional way.

Dobrota. Tel: (082) 322 521, (069) 220 455. Open: 8am–1am.

Konoba 'Stari Mlini' ★★

A top-notch traditional restaurant that has a great view of the bay. It's more than worth the trek.

Ljuta bb, Dobrota. Tel: (082) 333 555. www.starimlini.net. Open: 10am–midnight.

Skala Santa ★★

This charming and intimate restaurant in the old town of Kotor has a tasteful antique décor. The food is well prepared and served, and the wine list is very good. It's a perfect place for a romantic dinner. It is near the North Gate.

Stari Grad (Škaljarska Pjaca). Tel: (069) 299 836. Open: noon–midnight.

Ćatovića Mlini ★★★

A bit pricey, but this restaurant serves exceptional meat dishes and has very good service. It largely focuses on national cuisine but has a small selection of international dishes as well.

Morinj, Boka Kotorska. Tel: (082) 373 030. Fax: (082) 30 095. www.catovicamlini.com. Open: 11am–11pm.

ENTERTAINMENT

Diskoteka 'Maximus'

A multi-functional entertainment centre. Besides the main disco,

there is a piano bar, a nightclub and a daytime café. It's a classy but relaxed place.

Stari Grad, Trg od Oružja.

Forza Café

A bookstore, internet café and café rolled into one. It's in the main city square and is a perfect place to read the newspaper or write a few emails over morning coffee. There is a large terrace frequented daily by Podgorica's artists and writers. Exhibitions of local Montenegrin artists are frequently held here.

Trg od Oružja. Tel: (082) 304 352. Open: 7am–11pm.

Secondo Porto (Nightclub)

Places seem to fade in and out of popularity, but this club has remained the best in Boka Kotorska. The party goes on all night.

Škaljari bb. Open: 11pm–5am.

National Park Biogradska Gora

EATING OUT

Biogradsko Jezero ★★

A restaurant serving national food in the park.

It may seem like a pre-war relict, but the meat dishes are great and there are some excellent rural specialities.
Tel: (081) 865 625, (069) 032 621. Email: npbiogradskagora@cg.yu

Pljevlja
ACCOMMODATION
Gold ★
When travelling from Bosnia to Montenegro or vice versa, this is a convenient place for a rest in the small mountain town of Pljevlja.
M. Miljanova bb. Tel: (089) 323 102/103. Email: goldpv@cg.yu

EATING OUT
Milet Bašta ★★
This restaurant has a rustic atmosphere and serves traditional food and spirits.
Prvog Decembra bb. Tel: (067) 554 332.

Podgorica
ACCOMMODATION
Crna Gora ★★★
The hotel is a bit 'old school' with basic rooms, but nonetheless clean and comfortable. Located in the centre of town and 12km (7¹/₂ miles) from the airport.
Tel: (081) 634 271. Email: hotel@cg.yu

Eminent ★★★
One of Podgorica's most modern hotels.
The rooms and service are top quality and it's conveniently near the centre.
Njegoševa 25. Tel: (081) 664 545. Fax: (081) 664 273. Email: eminent@cg.yu. www.eminent.cg.yu

Kerber ★★★
Right in the centre of Podgorica, the Kerber claims to be one of the best hotels in town. The rooms are comfortable with a full range of services.
Novaka Miloševa 6. Tel: (081) 405 400/406. Email: hotelkerber@cg.yu. www.hotelkerber.cg.yu

EATING OUT
Kalabria ★★
This establishment specialises in Italian cuisine and has great salads and pasta dishes. The pizza is thought to be the best in town. The laidback atmosphere makes this a nice place to have a few beers with friends.
Marka Miljanova 61. Tel; (081) 622 577.

Mareza ★★
The specialities here are fresh trout, baked lamb and the best of Montenegro's wines. The service is friendly and professional, and the food is great.
Mareza bb. Tel: (081) 268 722. www.turizamcg.com. Open: 9am–1am.

Maša ★★★
Serving a good selection of international dishes and first-class sea fish, Maša is considered an institution in Podgorica.
Bulevar Svetog Petra Cetinjskog 7. Tel: (081) 224 460, 248 019. Open: 7am–midnight.

ENTERTAINMENT
Casino Crna Gora
Hotel Crna Gora, Bulevar Svetog Petra Cetinjskog. Tel: (081) 634 823, (067) 550 099. Open: 8pm–4am. www.casino-montenegro.com

Crnogorsko Narodno Pozorište (National Theatre of Montenegro)
Stanka Dragojevića 18. Tel: (081) 245 980, 242 647,

241 417. Fax: (081) 243 087.
Email: cnpm@cg.yu.
www.cnp.cg.yu
City Hall
This is an urban music
outlet. Used mostly as a
café during the day, there
are parties, discos and
regular live music
concerts in the evenings
and at night. The city's
Jazz Fest is held here
as well as summer
dance parties.
Njegošev Park.
Tel: (067) 222 888.
Open: 8am–2am.
Greenwich Caffe Bar
One of the best café bars
in Podgorica. This is a
favourite meeting place
with a great interior and
good music. It serves
a full range of drinks.
Check out the concert
schedule for good
local gigs.
Njegoševa 27. Tel: (067)
402 420, 383 333.
Email: greenwich@cg.yu.
Open: 8am–5am.
Kino Kultura (Kultura
Cinema)
IV Proleterske br.1.
Tel: (081) 230 557, (069)
022 187. Email:
bioskop.kultura@cg.yu.
www.kinokultura.cg.yu

Mr Good Café
Friendly staff and great
coffee make this one of
Podgorica's best and
most relaxing cafés.
Hercegovačka 33.
Tel: (067) 446 655, 232 042.
www.touristinmontenegro.
com

SPORT AND LEISURE
Montenegro Adventures
(Hiking and walking)
Moskovska (Maxim)
63–64. Tel: (069) 315 601,
(081) 244 228.
www.montenegro-
adventures.com
Savin Kuk (Snowboard
Club)
PO Box 400, Podgorica.
Tel: (069) 477 677.
Tennis Club Nec
Tel: (081) 652 504.
Turistička Agencija
(Discovery Tours)
(Cycling)
Tel: (081) 651 904.

Skadarsko Jezero
(Lake Skadar)
EATING OUT
Jezero ★
This restaurant serves
nothing but local
specialities caught in the
lake in front of you. Fresh,
home-made dishes.
Vranjina. Tel: (067) 619 603.

SPORT AND LEISURE
Lake Skadar (Boat rides)
10am departure and 4pm
return. Lunch is included
in the price.
Tel: (067) 256 557. Email:
jezero@turizamcg.com
Pelikan (Windsurfing)
Windsurfing on Lake
Skadar.
Vranjina, Skadarsko
Jezero. Tel: (069) 020 549,
424 013.

Sveti Stefan
ACCOMMODATION
Hotel-Castle Adrović ★★
One of the few less
expensive places in Sveti
Stefan. Set in a classic
Mediterranean
environment with a
baroque castle style, this
hotel is good value.
Jadranski Put bb, Sveti
Stefan. Tel: (086) 458 596,
468 876. Fax: (086) 458
312. Email:
hoteladrovic@cg.yu
Miločer ★★★
A former royal family
residence, the Miločer is.
fit for kings. It is
surrounded by lovely
parkland and the best
beach on Sveti Stefan.
It provides a full
range of quality
services.

Sveti Stefan, Miločer.
Tel: (086) 468 242.
Fax: (086) 468 242.
Email: brsales@cg.yu

Villa Montenegro ★★★

This villa is all about first-class travel with premium accommodation, fantastic service and all the creature comforts you could want or need.
Vukice Mitrović 2, Sveti Stefan. Tel: (086) 468 802.
Fax: (086) 468 809. Email: info@villa-montenegro.com.
www.villa-montenegro.com

EATING OUT
Drago ★★

Drago is proud of its delicious seafood and continental dishes. The lobster is fantastic, as are most things on the menu. It's a great deal for the price.
Ulica Slobode 32.
Tel: (086) 468 477/457.
Fax: (086) 468 477.
Email: petards@cg.yu

Kusta ★★

Halfway between Budva and Hotel Miločer on Sveti Stefan is Kusta. It specialises in grilled meats and has a hardy mixed grill special.

Sveti Stefan Par. 340, Budva.
Tel: (069) 403 722.

ENTERTAINMENT
Casino Hotel Sveti Stefan

This late-night venue has gambling, of course, but music and entertainment on occasion as well
Tel: (086) 468 118.
Open: 8pm–5am.

Ulcinj
ACCOMMODATION
Hotel Dvori Balšića ★★

Located between the ancient city walls in Ulcinj old town, this 14th-century former king's residence is one of two hotels that have been transformed from royal residences to tourist accommodation. Dvori Balšića has luxury apartments with all the modernities but with a rustic touch.
Stari Grad.
Tel: (085) 421 457.
Email: realestate@cg.yu

Palata Venecija ★★

These former king's quarters have been transformed into a first-class hotel. The charming building

near the city walls in the old town is perfect for experiencing the town as Montenegro's rulers once did.
Stari Grad.
Tel: (085) 421 457.

EATING OUT
Miško ★★

The oldest restaurant in the Bojana delta has a long tradition of good fish dishes. The décor may seem odd, but the food certainly isn't.
Ada Bojana.
Tel: (069) 022 868.
Open: 10am–midnight.

Riblja Čorba ★★

Riblja Čorba means 'fish stew' and the dish here is excellent.
Ada Bojana.
Tel: (069) 032 517.

SPORT AND LEISURE
D'Olcinium (Diving)

Active and extreme diving and diving lessons and gear in Ulcinj. Great location for scuba diving around Ada Bojana.
Tel: (067) 319 100.
Email: realstate@cg.yu.
www.uldiving.com

Žabljak

ACCOMMODATION

Enigma ★
This tiny hotel is new with basic but modern facilities. It is about 1km (²/₃ mile) from the town centre.
Tel: (069) 598 555, (089) 360 130/131. Email: hotelenigma@cg.yu

Javor ★
This is a pre-war hotel in the centre of Žabljak. It offers basic but good services in a good location.
Bočidara Žugića 8.
Tel: (089) 361 337.
Fax: (089) 361 307.
Email: hotel-javor@ hotmail.com.
www.durmitor.org.yu

Jezera ★
This is the main hotel for the ski centre, with over 200 beds. It is found between Žabljak town and Crno Lake. It also offers villas (which are more like bungalows) that can sleep two to four people; perfect for families or small hiking groups if you want to cook for yourself.
Tel: (089) 360 204.
Fax: (089) 89 360 205.
hmdurmitor@hotmail.com

EATING OUT

Restoran 'Javorovača' ★
For those who like open fire grills and delicious mountain dishes, this is the mountain's best highland food. Thick stews, tasty cheeses, and high-quality beef and lamb are definitely worth a long dinner session to try and fit them all in.
Naselje Javorovača.
Tel: (089) 360 236/237,
(069) 020 701.
Email: corma@cg.yu.
Open: 8am–11pm.

SPORT AND LEISURE

Agencija Sveti Dordije (Skiing)
Tel: (089) 61 367.

Durmitor National Park (Rafting)
Tel: (089) 61 346/474.

NGO 'MOST' (Hiking and walking)
Vučedolska bb.
Tel: (089) 360 010, (067) 227 228.
Fax: (089) 360 010.
Email: hitss@cg.yu.
www.ngo-most.org

Skijaški Savez Crne Gore (Skiing Association of Montenegro)
Danila Bojovića 3, Nikšić.
Tel: (083) 244 649.

Turistička Agencija (Tara River Tours)
This operator offers organised white-water adventures of one to three days on the Tara River.
Tel: (083) 271 359.

Žabljak Ski Centar (Skiing)
The main ski centre in Montenegro in Durmitor National Park.
Tel: (089) 61 144.

Index

Acknowledgements

The author would like to give special thanks to Sanela and Adnan Prekic for their help and knowledge. The following institutions were key factors in helping research this book: USAID, Tourism Organization of Montenegro, Canton Sarajevo Tourism Association, Federation of BiH Tourism Association. Their assistance in helping create this guide is greatly appreciated.

Thomas Cook Publishing wishes to thank the following photographers, libraries and associations for their assistance in the preparation of this book, to whom the copyright in the photographs belongs:

TIM CLANCY 5, 8, 27, 30, 33, 44, 45, 47, 52, 56, 62, 97, 104, 112, 128, 131, 134, 135, 147; TOURISM ORGANIZATION OF MONTENEGRO (MUNEVER SALIHOVIC, SANELA PREKIC, ADNAN PREKIC) 9, 69, 71, 75, 77, 78, 79, 81, 83, 84, 85, 91, 103, 106, 107, 109, 111, 119, 136, 137, 138; WIKIMEDIA COMMONS 23, 25, 29 (CHRISTIAN BICKEL), 34, 36, 37, 38, 48 (CrniBombarder!!!), 50 (NAPOLEON SARONY), 55 (SVETLANA I MIRKO), 57 (WOLFGANG HUNSCHER), 58, 65 (HERBERT ORTNER), 67 (CrniBombarder!!!), 73 (ANNA PRZYBYSZEWSKA), 82 (VLADO VUJISIC), 86, 87 (MAZBIN), 88 (MAZBIN), 89 (MAZBIN), 92, 99, 100, 115 (HERBERT ORTNER), 125, 129, 142, 143 (NATIONAL BANK OF SERBIA); PICTURES COLOUR LIBRARY 31, 72, 117, 130; MUNEVER SALIHOVIC 32, 35, 40; DREAMSTIME.COM/SELMA HODZIC 43; WORLD PICTURES 60, 61, 108, 110, 116, 140; FOTOLIA/VLADO MARINKOVIC 63; ZDENKO MARIC 93; CARLY CALHOUN 98, 132; SEBASTIEN VENUAT 94, 102; VLADO MARINKOVIC 13, 15, 118, 127

Copy-editing: JO OSBORN for CAMBRIDGE PUBLISHING MANAGEMENT LTD

Index: KAROLIN THOMAS for CAMBRIDGE PUBLISHING MANAGEMENT LTD

Maps: PC GRAPHICS, Old Woking, UK

Proofreading: IAN FAULKNER for CAMBRIDGE PUBLISHING MANAGEMENT LTD

SEND YOUR THOUGHTS TO
BOOKS@THOMASCOOK.COM

We're committed to providing the very best up-to-date information in our travel guides and constantly strive to make them as useful as they can be. You can help us to improve future editions by letting us have your feedback. If you've made a wonderful discovery on your travels that we don't already feature, if you'd like to inform us about recent changes to anything that we do include, or if you simply want to let us know your thoughts about this guidebook and how we can make it even better – we'd love to hear from you.

Send us ideas, discoveries and recommendations today and then look out for your valuable input in the next edition of this title.

Emails to the above address, or letters to Travellers Project Editor, Thomas Cook Publishing, PO Box 227, Coningsby Road, Peterborough PE3 8SB, UK.

Please don't forget to let us know which title your feedback refers to!